KNIGHT BREW

THE BARKS & BEANS CAFE MYSTERY SERIES
BOOK 9

HEATHER DAY GILBERT

Knight Brew

Copyright 2024 Heather Day Gilbert

Cover Design by Elizabeth Mackey of Elizabeth Mackey Graphics

Published by WoodHaven Press

This book is a work of fiction. Any references to historical events, real people, or real places are used fictitiously. Other names, characters, places, and events are products of the author's imagination, and any resemblance to actual events or places or persons living or dead is entirely coincidental.

Series: Gilbert, Heather Day. Barks & Beans Cafe Mystery; 9

Subject: Detective and Mystery Stories; Coffeehouses—Fiction; Dogs —Fiction Genre: Mystery Fiction

Author Information & Newsletter: http://www. heatherdaygilbert.com

FROM THE BACK COVER

Book Nine in the RWA Daphne Award-winning series!

Welcome to the Barks & Beans Cafe, a quaint place where folks pet shelter dogs while enjoying a cup of java...and where murder sometimes pays a visit.

The Barks & Beans booth at the Renaissance Faire is hopping, since Macy managed to talk her muscled redhead brother into donning a kilt for the occasion. Even better, Macy's boyfriend Titan has come for a visit, so she can't wait to peruse the shops and watch the shows with him.

But when a well-rehearsed joust takes a fatal turn, Macy becomes a key witness. Can she believe her eyes, or did someone cloak their ruthless intent with smoke and mirrors? A late night stakeout seems the only way to determine what really happened...but someone scarier than the plague doctor is lying in wait for Macy, and this time, the damsel might not find a way out of her distress.

Join siblings Macy and Bo Hatfield as they sniff out crimes in their hometown...with plenty of dogs along for the ride! The Barks & Beans Cafe cozy mystery series features a small town, an amateur sleuth, and no swearing or graphic scenes. Find all the books at heatherdaygilbert.com!

The Barks & Beans Cafe series in order:

Dedicated to Aunt Tonya, who enjoyed my books and trusted God's plan for her life, even when cancer became a part of it. Her smile and her zest for life were contagious, and she will be greatly missed until we see her again someday.

1

As I took a huge bite of my Italian sub, my Great Dane Coal licked his lips, but managed to keep himself firmly planted at the top of my brother's back deck steps. He was aware that if he intruded on our meal, I'd put him inside, where Bo's incorrigible calico Stormy was anxiously awaiting her chance to pounce on his tail.

Bo's fiancée Summer leaned back and heaved a satisfied sigh. "I'll tell you what—those turkey subs on parmesan bread are the *best*. I can't believe I put that whole thing away."

Bo looked duly impressed at Summer's feat. "I'm glad you liked it. Who knew you were such a sub fiend? I couldn't finish more than three-fourths of mine."

My boyfriend Titan wiped his mouth. He'd actually finished his entire sub and about a third mine on top of that, but he was six-foot-five, so it took a lot to fill his tank. "Those were great, Bo." He leaned back in the turquoise rocking chair he'd pulled up beside me, since it was tricky for him to slide his long limbs under the picnic table. "Is everything set up for the Barks & Beans booth at the Ren Faire tomorrow? I can't wait to drop by—and for Macy to see my costume." He shot me a wink.

"Shouldn't be too much left to do," Bo said. "Charity pre-wraps all her gourmet sandwiches and desserts, so those are no-mess. And we have a limited—but exciting—selection of coffee drinks."

Summer grinned. "Why do I feel like I'm being sold a bill of goods? But I have tried a couple of those drinks, and you're not exaggerating. They're some of your best concoctions yet. I think my fave is the Wild Wizard. So much cinnamon."

"Mine's the Jester's Java," I said. "An iced raspberry latte with fresh raspberries on top."

Titan frowned. "Do you have anything a little less frou-frou?" he asked. "I'm basically a ham-and-egger."

That was something I liked about him—he was just as eager to eat a supper of chicken tenders from my freezer as he was the handmade spinach ravioli my brother whipped up every now and then. "Since you like our Irish Cream Latte, you'd probably enjoy the Knight Brew," I said, folding the wrapper around my sub leftovers. "It has rum extract, brown sugar, and vanilla ice cream. There are a few silver sprinkles thrown on top, mind you."

He nodded, and one of his dark curls dropped over

an eye. He'd told me he needed a hair trim, but I found his long curls infinitely fascinating. Not to mention the maple-colored eyes they framed. "That's definitely up my alley," he said. "You know me well."

Summer turned to me. "How's that new kid doing at the cafe? You think he'll be able to replace Bristol when she heads to art school this fall?"

"His name's August Blackwell, and he's hardly a new kid on the block. He's in his late twenties, and he grew up around here," I explained. "And I don't really know yet. He seems to have the barista angle down, but he hasn't spent much time in the Barks section. He did get along fine with Coal during his interview, so I'm assuming he's good with dogs, like he said. And since Bristol recommended him as a family friend, I figure he'll work out fine."

"I'm just glad you hired someone. That'll be a load off your mind come fall," she said. "I'm short-staffed at the shelter, and we've already hit maximum capacity a couple of times this summer. I'm hoping things will calm down soon, especially since we're getting married in October." She reached out, placing her tan hand over Bo's freckled one. Her engagement ring twinkled in the fading sunlight.

My brother's sky-blue eyes softened. "That we are."

It was good to see his vulnerable side peeking out. Summer had singlehandedly restored his hope in womankind, effectively healing the emotional damage he'd experienced from a broken engagement. He hadn't mentioned his ex-fiancée Tara for months, so I had to believe he'd finally put her unexpected rejection —and her lingering influence—behind him.

"I can't believe you're going to meet my family soon." Summer's voice cracked, and she squeezed Bo's hand harder. Even in that small gesture, her unspoken grief seemed to roll my way. She had been estranged from her Mennonite family for years, but she'd never told me why. I'd always guessed it had something to do with her strong independent streak—she did have purple hair when I met her, although now it was back to its natural caramel color. I couldn't imagine her taking kindly to a bunch of rigid rules.

Yet she always spoke fondly of her four younger brothers, and I knew she called her parents on their community phone on holidays. She'd moved quite a distance to escape her Pennsylvania home, so it would be a long trip when she and Bo drove up to pay her family a visit.

Given the understanding look on Bo's face, I figured she'd filled him in on her past. She would likely put me in the loop someday, since she was basically my sister at this point.

"I'm glad to go there with you," Bo said. "Family is important."

I stretched my arms along the picnic table. "I'm feeling all fat and happy after that food. Now it's time for Coal's supper."

Coal turned his pricked ears my way. He was waiting for me to say the magic word: "Home."

I grabbed my sub and motioned for him to follow.

"Let's get home, boy. Titan, do you want to hang out awhile at my place?"

My boyfriend stood up next to me. Even though I felt tiny next to him at five-foot-three, I also felt protected, like a delicate bird's nest tucked into a sturdy maple limb. He wrapped a long arm around my shoulder. "I'll walk you over, but then I'd better get back to the cabin. I wish they'd get a dishwasher in there, since I'm constantly doing dishes. But overall, it's a relaxing place to stay. You should drop by—they've finally replaced that leaky rowboat. Now they have a tandem kayak that's pretty comfortable on the pond."

"That sounds lovely." I recalled the comforting wood smoke smell of the rustic cabin Titan liked to rent when he was in. In those pine woods, I felt like I had all the time in the world to enjoy both nature and uninterrupted conversation.

Bo stood and gave Titan a powerful clap on the back. "Thanks for coming over, brother. We'll see you tomorrow, then." He rolled his eyes. "Wait'll you get a load of the outfit Macy picked out for me."

I grinned at Summer, since she'd given her full approval to the navy plaid kilt, leather sporran bag, and Henley shirt I'd chosen for Bo's faire costume. He'd obligingly grown his red beard and hair out to look a little rougher around the edges, and Summer told me she hoped he'd keep it that way for the wedding. "It looks like he's stepped off the heather Highlands with an axe to grind," she said. "He's irresistible when he looks dangerous."

I figured he'd have the same effect on the females at the fairgrounds, which would likely increase foot traffic to our cafe booth. I was nothing if not mercenary when it came to exploiting my brother's rugged good looks for monetary gain. Besides, his heart belonged to Summer, and she enjoyed the full confidence that he wouldn't so much as flirt with another woman.

Bo was, in fact, the complete opposite of my ex-husband Jake, who couldn't stop smiling when attractive women so much as glanced his way. Why I didn't see through his cheating ways earlier, I'd never know.

Titan pulled me back into the moment with a tentative half-smile, as if he guessed I was pondering painful things. He was another man whose heart was loyal, but I hadn't yet allowed myself to feel the full weight of that fact. He'd said he was hoping for marriage, but he wouldn't propose until he believed I was ready to take that step.

I tucked one arm under his, clenching my uneaten sub in my free hand. "Love you, bro. See you soon, Summer."

Coal lumbered through the door behind us, pausing briefly in order to lean down and acknowledge Stormy. The fluffy cat promptly swiped at his nose with her paw.

"You're a real lulu, you know that?" I asked her. "Come on, Coal."

WE WALKED down the sidewalk past Titan's SUV, then opened the gate into my back garden, which was starting to fill out with hostas, hollyhocks, and roses. My great-aunt Athaleen had worked hard to build these flowerbeds, and I'd found it surprisingly invigorating to putter around in them since I'd moved in.

When we reached my door, Titan smiled. "My mom is so excited that you're coming up for July fourth. She was so impressed to meet you and see the cafe over Christmas. Dad and my sisters can't wait to meet you, too."

"And Granny McCoy?" I asked. "Have you broken the news that I'm a loathsome Hatfield yet?"

He shook his head. "What she doesn't know won't hurt her. I want her to get a feel of who you are first, then she can find out who you're kin to. She has her guest room all set up for you."

I swallowed my nervousness, trying to pretend I wasn't concerned. If Granny McCoy didn't approve of me—which was certainly possible given her lifelong contempt for the Hatfield family—I could lose some serious traction with Titan's family. From what I understood, his granny was a regular matriarch along the lines of Auntie A, and those women were not to be taken lightly. They were the ones who shaped the world to come, often with their prayers alone.

He gave me a warm look and took my hand in his. "I don't want you worrying about Granny. She's a smart woman, just like you. She's going to love you, like I do."

It was still strange to hear him admitting his love

for me. He stepped closer to give me a thoughtful kiss, and I tasted a trace of salt on his lips. "Have a good night, Macy," he said, his voice a bit rough. "I hope you recognize me tomorrow."

He was so excited about surprising me with his mysterious costume. I'd already told him I was wearing Viking garb, which he'd deemed to be a good choice. But he had adamantly refused to divulge what his cosplay plans were.

"I'll be watching for your grand appearance," I said.

He gave me a parting hug and walked down the steps, and I pushed the door open for Coal. He made a beeline for his empty food dish, so I stashed my sub in the fridge and fed him.

When I curled up on the couch a little later, he padded over, hoping to sit next to me. I patted the cushion and he clambered up, stretching out along my feet. I patted his sleek black head and started talking to him, as was my habit. "I don't know what I'll do if his granny disapproves of me," I said. "Because there's no way I'm walking away from Titan McCoy."

Coal angled his head and gave me a concerned look, as if he, too, hoped for a good outcome with Granny McCoy.

There was nothing on earth quite like a loyal dog who'd be willing to walk through fire for you, should the need arise. I leaned over and gave Coal a big hug. "Then we could all be one big, happy family."

2

I pulled out the brown, aproned Viking dress from my closet, irritated to see that the packing wrinkles had yet to fall out. Such was the nature of linen, I supposed.

After rummaging around in Auntie A's jewelry box, I managed to turn up a wood-beaded necklace that looked somewhat Medieval, so I added it to my costume. Then I slid on a thick leather belt before heading to the bathroom, where I wove a few small braids to my fluffy strawberry-blonde mane. With my brown eyeliner, I drew thick streaks along my cheeks, hoping they looked more warrior than street urchin. Once I'd added an ornate silver earring and slid into my comfiest leather boots, I felt ready to face the world as a Viking maiden.

It was a quick trip to the Renaissance fairground. Vendors were traipsing across the dewy grass parking lot with their wares. Bo had already parked his truck up near the treeline, which came as no surprise to me. He was chronically early, since he liked to have time to familiarize himself with the layout of any given locale —probably harking back to his days in the DEA and, earlier, in the Marines.

Regardless, my brother always seemed ready for anything. I couldn't say the same for myself, but I liked to think that my ability to play things by ear was one of my biggest strengths.

The cloudless sky promised a lovely but hot summer day, and I hoped my layered linen dress and boots wouldn't get me too sweaty by the end of it. I didn't have much to do at our booth, since making coffee drinks wasn't my forte. Instead, my job was to ring up the food and hand out photo cards Summer had given me, featuring current shelter animals. I had to chuckle at the names they'd recently assigned to the dogs, which were based on characters from the *Psych* TV show. This included Jules, Gus, Shawn, and my personal favorite—a sad-looking hound named Lassiter.

It was easy to spot our booth, which was close to the gates. We'd calculated that it might prove advanta-geous to set up away from the food court area, for those who didn't care for eating in a crowd. We had a couple of wooden benches near our white-canopied booth, where people could sit and "take a load off," as Auntie A used to say.

Bo was stacking cups on the counter. From the top of his ginger head to his folded-top knee socks, he looked like a Scottish laird ready to defend his castle. But he wasn't wearing the Henley shirt we'd bought for him. Instead, he'd donned a green tee that showed his upper arm tattoo.

He followed my questioning gaze. "I'm sorry, sis, but there's no way I could've worn that long-sleeved shirt today. But I'll use that shirt come fall, so thanks for buying it for me. Also, you look quite fierce."

"Oh, thank you, and no problem on the shirt. I hope a breeze will pick up, otherwise this muggy air is going to be stifling today. At least we're situated near a shade tree. I can't imagine being out in the blazing sun in that food court."

He nodded. "Hey, did you get any coffee yet?" He was always willing to brew me a cup, and it was always outstanding.

" I did—I had one of those hazelnut coffee pods, just to get some caffcine into my system. They aren't the best, but I've run out of our house blend."

Bo made a disgusted face. "Tell me you didn't dump creamer in on top of it."

Before I could respond to his snide remark, I noticed that our new employee August was making his way toward us. He wore a green, hooded shirt and brown pants and carried a bow, and he had a quiver of arrows strapped on his back.

"Robin Hood?" I guessed.

He gave me a slight grin. "William Tell." He deposited his bow onto the chair behind the counter, leaving the quiver on his back. "I like to be eclectic. It's actually a really touching Swiss story, one my grand-mother used to read to me when I was small."

It wasn't that surprising that August had chosen something bookish. Given what Bristol had told me when she'd recommended him, he was the dark and brooding type who enjoyed writing poetry and lurking in coffee shops. The barista job would help him pay for trade school, where he was currently studying forensic investigation.

August asked if Bo could walk him through making a Thor's Hammer iced coffee one more time, since it was a bit trickier with the double espresso base. As the men got to work, I arranged Summer's shelter cards and glanced at the neighboring booths.

Arlo Edwards, owner of the cute Recycled Reads bookshop, had set up a couple of booths beyond ours. I caught his eye and he touched his head, giving me a half bow. He was a charming, well-read man with long blond hair, a beard, and decidedly hippie tendencies. Even though he was probably in his mid-40s, he'd always struck me as a lot older than my own forty years. I made a mental note to drop by his booth and ask if he had any antique copies of *Sense and Sensibility* —I was a huge Colonel Brandon fan.

Once the gates finally opened and the Medieval tavern music started piping through the loudspeakers, it didn't take long for our booth to start hopping. The customer demographic skewed largely toward single women who were lining up to place their orders with Bo. August didn't seem offended that his line was much shorter, and besides, Bo was born for a frenetic pace. Together, we made a solid team.

While several customers seemed interested in the shelter photo cards, a couple people let them flutter to the ground on their way out. I'd forgotten how messy fairgrounds could be. I added trash pickup to my list of duties at the booth.

Bo gave a slight groan, and I followed his gaze toward my neighbor Vera, who was walking her troublemaking Labradoodle Waffles our way. Waffles had a history of going bonkers during her stints in the doggie section at the cafe, so my brother was likely dreading a repeat performance.

My eyes widened as I took in Vera's outfit, which was the most un-Vera look imaginable. She wore a sequined blouse from the eighties, a long floral skirt topped with a pink tutu, and a pair of gold slingback flats. Adding to her mismatched look, she'd tucked a fake orange hibiscus flower into her cropped white hair.

As I greeted Vera, Waffles strained at her leash to say hello. Her curly blond tail beat circles in the air, and she wriggled with delight to see me. Her vacuous brown eyes gazed into mine, as if willing me to pet her.

Bo shot the dog a warning look that was completely wasted on her.

"You look fancy today," I said, hoping my neighbor might explain her creative getup.

"Why, thank you." Vera pulled Waffles into a sitting position, and Bo visibly relaxed. "I hadn't planned on dressing up, but Randall told me it was par for the course here. I'm going to drop in at his leatherworking booth, so I can look for something for my son's birthday." She gave a playful half-twirl, causing Waffles to release a nervous yip. "I'm Titania, of course." She adjusted the hibiscus in her hair. "From *Midsummer Night's Dream.*"

Now her whimsical outfit was starting to make sense. "How clever," I said. "I'm a Viking, and we also have William Tell and a Scottish warrior." I gestured toward Bo and August.

Vera's gaze traveled over the men. "A goodly company indeed. Well, Waffles and I had better head over to see Randall. Is Titan coming by today?"

My neighbor found Titan endlessly fascinating, largely because he was tall, dark, and handsome. She'd also let drop that if he married me, she'd have both him and Bo nearby to help with any repairs she needed. A two-man army of able-bodied men, ready to aid their widowed neighbor woman.

"He's dropping in around lunch, since I have to work until then," I explained.

"Well, you two enjoy the faire. I know I intend to," she said, her voice unusually chipper.

As she led Waffles away, I had to stare after her— the Queen of the Fairies seemed such an incongruous costume choice for my down-to-earth neighbor. Her late-in-life romance with Randall Mathena had certainly brought out her wild side. It was refreshing to see Vera getting out and relishing her life with her boyfriend, the same way I was with mine.

THE UNRELENTING SUN was high in the sky, and I'd started to feel famished. As I turned from placing the oatmilk in the fridge, a tall knight clanked into view. His black armor and helmet gave him an ominous look, and he headed straight to my side of the counter.

Bo had his back to the knight as he made an iced coffee for a customer, so he didn't notice him. August, who should be the one to take his order, took a step closer.

The knight stayed focused on me and cleared his throat. "I'd like a medium Knight Brew, my lady."

The moment I recognized his deep voice, I relaxed. "Titan! Your costume is impressive." As he rested his metal-clad arms on the counter, I asked, "How on earth did you manage to fit your head into that tiny helmet?"

He obligingly placed both hands on the sides of his helmet and wrenched it off. His sweat-dampened curls stuck to his forehead, and his cheeks were red. "Good question. I had to buy a new costume, since the one from high school was too small. Apparently, I've had a serious growth spurt since my last visit to Medieval World. But the armor I ordered didn't come with a helmet, so I had to squeeze into my old one." He managed a grin. "Anything for my lady."

"Your lady would be happier if you didn't get your

head stuck in there," I said. "How about you take that off while we get our lunch?"

"Gladly." He took the Knight Brew from August, who had whipped it up while we were chatting. "Thanks," he said, sipping at the silver-sprinkled ice cream topping. Once he'd gotten a decent sip of the coffee beneath, he grinned. "This stuff is amazing, especially on a hot day." He extended a hand toward August. "You must be the new barista-slash-dog wrangler."

August nodded. "That I am, sir. August Blackwell, at your service."

"Titan McCoy, Macy's boyfriend. You've certainly got a good touch with the coffee drinks."

"Thank you, sir."

I found it cute the way August kept calling Titan "sir." But before I could comment on it, another knight veered from the path and came straight toward the counter. He carried a half-eaten kielbasa that was slathered in ketchup.

After looking up at Titan, he gave him a slap on his metal shoulder plating. "You ready for combat, mate? I don't recall seeing you at practice yesterday."

When Titan gave him a confused look, I hurried to set the record straight. "He's not a jouster. I take it you are?"

The thirty-something man nodded, turning his full attention toward me. He was what some would consider good-looking, albeit in a world-weary way.

"Indeed I am, shieldmaiden. I've already won a joust today, and I aim to win another."

I could almost feel Titan bristling at the man's cloying tone, but the knight continued his quest to impress me. "I've worked up a fearsome thirst. Have ye something to recommend that could slake my violent need?"

August thoughtfully stepped in, drawing the man's attention his way. "I'd recommend an iced chai latte, sir. It's got a perfect kick, but goes down smooth."

"Hit me with that one, young fry." He turned back to me and leered. "My name is Robbie Sears, little lady."

Titan took a big gulp of coffee, as if bracing himself for a throw-down with the obnoxious knight.

Robbie's attention was suddenly diverted by a woman who stalked up to him. She wore black leather pants and a ruffled red blouse, and her dark hair was slicked back into a tight bun.

She punched Robbie's armored arm so hard he actually winced. "Do you feel ready to joust with Eli? He's been looking forward to knocking some sense into you."

He shrugged, then gave her a smirk. "I reckon I could take that peasant in my sleep."

She snorted, blinking her heavily-lined eyes at him. Her sleeveless blouse revealed her belly button, and metal armbands circled her slim wrists. Was she some type of Flamenco dancer?

"I've seen your practice runs, remember?" she spat

out. "Your horseback skills don't hold a candle to Eli's, you poser."

Bo had now turned his full attention to the situation, which meant that the woman had definitely overstepped. August quickly intervened, reaching over and handing Robbie his iced latte.

The knight reluctantly slapped a ten-dollar bill on the counter as the woman stamped off. After taking a sip, Robbie declared, "'Tis a goodly brew, my boy." He grabbed his change, then crudely shoved the large, ketchup-dripping piece of kielbasa in his mouth. As he strode off, his plate metal scraped together, creating a noise as unbearable as nails on a chalkboard.

Arlo, who must've witnessed the entire heated exchange, hurried over to our counter. "That guy is trouble," he said quietly. "I caught him trying to steal a signed copy of Brad Thor's latest release from my table. He denied it, but he was holding the book behind his back. He would've walked off with it if I hadn't turned around."

"Do you know the story between him and the lady in the red blouse?" I asked.

He nodded. "That's his ex-wife Cora—she's a trick rider, and one of the best. Her new husband is Eli, and he's a jouster, too, so that makes things incredibly awkward on the fairground. I heard that when she was married to Robbie, she helped him run his horse breeding business, but when they divorced, she got no part of it. She found out that he co-owned the business with his second wife, so she really seems to hate him now."

"Wait—how many wives has he had?" I asked.

"As far as I can count, there have been three, but Vera might know better," Arlo said. He gave Titan a respectful nod. "Glad you're in for a visit."

Titan seemed surprised at the greeting, since he hadn't officially met Arlo yet, but he gave him a polite smile. He seemed distracted, and I felt certain that Robbie had gotten under his skin.

"Let's get some lunch," I suggested, stepping out from behind the counter and sliding my arm under his. "But you'd better stash that sad helmet here."

3

Titan seemed to unwind as we made a circuit of the packed fairground. We dropped by Randall's booth, but he told us that Vera and Waffles had already headed into the fairy forest. After taking some time to examine Randall's beautifully crafted leather goods, I finally bought an embossed change purse.

I glanced at the purple tent sitting directly across from his booth. Wind chimes dangled from its mesh awning, and a painted sign reading "Let Cosmic Crystal Tell Your Future" sat propped against the front table.

Robbie the knight was standing under the awning, talking with a seated woman I assumed to be Crystal.

She was predictably wearing a turban, along with a tiered, multicolored skirt that gave her a gypsy look. Her armful of bracelets jangled each time she moved, and she jabbed at the air as she spoke. She was clearly upset.

Robbie maintained an amused expression as he sipped on the remainder of his iced chai latte. Crystal got increasingly worked up, and I caught her saying the word "cards."

Just as I was considering moving closer to her tent, Titan started walking toward the food court. I had to hurry to keep up with his long strides, so I put the fortune-teller out of my mind.

We sidestepped the free-range chickens to wait in line for the Caribbean chicken sandwiches we'd heard good things about. Once we finally got them, along with Titan's order of cheese curds, I suggested that we head up to the fairy forest to find a place to eat in the shade. Titan readily agreed, and as we walked up the hill, we noticed Robbie had already segued over to the mermaid lagoon, where he seemed to be flirting with an uncomfortable Ariel.

"You've got to be kidding me," I muttered. "Who does he think he is?"

"A valiant knight, I suppose," His lips twisted into a frown. "He isn't worthy of the role."

We passed several beautifully costumed fairies who fluttered around us, then retreated toward an open barn where a Celtic group called The Frazier Five was singing. Titan tried to ease onto a picnic table bench, but neither his armor nor his legs would allow him to squeeze under the tabletop. He sat down backward instead, with his legs outstretched. Trying to keep a straight face for my Tin Man, I joined him in the same position and positioned my lunch in my lap.

"I always forget how difficult it is to enjoy your food at fairs," I said. "The heat doesn't help, either." I glanced at him, knowing he had to be sweltering in his knight costume, but he maintained his stoic posture.

While his FBI training would've prepared him for far worse situations than lumbering around in a heavy metal costume in the heat of summer, his patience spoke volumes about his determination to impress me. He'd deliberately chosen a knight costume—maybe a nod to his being my knight in shining armor?—and there was no one I'd rather hang out with in my free time.

After about fifteen minutes, The Frazier Five put down their bagpipes to take a break, so we decided to dump our food trash and make our way back to the Barks & Beans booth. We wandered past the fairies, who had abandoned their positions to cluster together in their tent.

Something had clearly happened. Several of the fairies spoke anxiously as all eyes centered on a redheaded fairy in a topaz-colored dress. When another fairy in a sparkling red mask placed an arm around the topaz fairy, she promptly started sobbing.

Concerned about the young woman, I took a few steps closer to ask if I could help, but the fairies closed ranks, completely blocking me. Apparently, they didn't want any fairgoers getting involved.

I returned to Titan, who'd been waiting on the outskirts of the circle, and he silently took my arm, leading me away from the perplexing scene. I told myself the fairies could look after themselves, even though I worried about what might have brought the topaz fairy to tears.

A trumpet blew, then a man announced that the joust would begin in five minutes. We edged around the back of the joust ring, which offered me a clear view of Robbie, who was taking a swig from a green water bottle. He saw me and winked, but luckily Titan was looking at the royalty sitting in the raised box on the opposite side.

Cora also stood on the opposing side, alongside a knight I presumed to be her new husband Eli. I certainly hoped he would win, so he could take Sir Robbie down a notch.

A shorter knight walked a black horse over to Robbie. He took the water bottle, then helped Robbie climb onto the saddle. Robbie promptly trotted onto the field and shouted a few Medieval taunts at Eli, who fired back—aided by Cora, who shouted some words that definitely weren't fit for the younger ears in the crowd. Clearly, this joust was personal to her.

The trumpet gave a short blast, and the horses charged toward each other. Both men had their lances out and shields up, although Robbie's lance seemed to be drooping a little. Titan led me to a closer spot, so I could better see the middle space where they would meet up.

Eli landed the first blow, causing Robbie to totter, but the horses continued galloping until they reached their respective sides of the ring. Robbie was sagging in his saddle, which hardly seemed like good form. Cora was right—he didn't have half the style of Eli on horseback, so why did he act like some kind of hot stuff knight?

The horses wheeled around, and the knights made a second run at each other. This time, Eli's blow landed squarely into Robbie's shield, but to everyone's horror, Robbie completely toppled off his horse. Eli's horse reared up, then came down on Robbie's leg, causing a hideous cracking sound.

Screams broke out, and the fortune-teller Crystal burst from the crowd, yelling Robbie's name. Titan was already moving toward the injured man, so I hurried after him. Crystal knelt by Robbie's side, smacking at his face, but his eyes were closed.

Titan was about to check for a pulse when Doctor Stan Stokes reached us. "They called me over," he said breathlessly. "I'll check him."

I explained that Doc Stokes was my family practice doctor growing up, and Titan was only too happy to step aside in the face of his expertise. The doctor checked for a pulse. "Thready," he declared, then leaned down to listen for breathing sounds. "He's in respiratory arrest. Might be an overdose." He pulled his keychain out of his pocket, which had a collapsible face shield to protect him from drug contamination. Looking at Titan, he said, "I'll do CPR breaths if you do the chest compressions. You'll have more strength than I do."

Titan agreed, and together, the men worked to

bring Robbie back to consciousness. Crystal hunkered next to them, tears streaming down her face.

I stood and shouted, "Has anyone called EMS?"

People shot me hopeless looks, although one man said he'd called 9-1-1. I was pulling out my own phone when Bo came jogging into the joust ring.

"Hey, sis. I've sent August to get the paramedics parked outside the gate." He waved his arms and yelled, "The show's over, everyone! Please disperse so the ambulance can get through."

"He's breathing again," the doctor said suddenly.

Titan stopped his compressions, allowing the doctor to monitor Robbie's vital signs. When Doctor Stokes gave a relieved sigh, so did I.

With the tenuous situation somewhat in-hand, I knelt by the weeping fortune-teller and gave her a pat on the back. "I'm so sorry, Crystal—were you and Robbie close?"

She gave me a confused look, then understanding crossed her face. "Oh—my name's not really Crystal." She dabbed a balled-up tissue at her eyes. "It's Deanna. And yes, he was my husband. I mean, he's my ex now, but we're still good friends."

Speaking of exes, Cora was nowhere in sight, and neither was her new husband Eli, who'd been the one to knock Robbie off his horse. Why hadn't they stuck around to see if Robbie was okay? Were they really that callous?

The ambulance siren sounded a couple of times before the vehicle eased up onto the nearby grass.

Paramedics spilled out, then loaded Robbie onto a stretcher and hurried him into the waiting vehicle. As Titan helped Doctor Stokes to his feet, Deanna edged over and gripped the doctor's arm.

"Is he breathing steady now? Is he going to be okay?" she asked.

The doctor gave her a comforting smile and patted her hand. "He's breathing, yes. And he's in good hands." He gave me a nod and thanked Titan for his help, then walked over to rejoin his family, who were waiting on the hillside.

A police officer arrived, presumably because of the possible overdose situation. Bo greeted him and started filling him in, then Titan headed over to join them.

Deanna gave a sniff. Her eyeliner and mascara had streaked, leaving black rivulets down her cheeks, so I fished a clean tissue from my pocket and handed it to her.

"Thank you," she said gratefully. "I told Robbie that calamity was going to enter his life soon. I saw something dark coming in the cards. But he just laughed it off and said I should stop taking my Cosmic Crystal role so seriously."

As she launched into a fresh round of tears, I suggested, "Why don't I walk you back to your tent? It's so sunny out here, and I'm sure you could use something to drink. I'd be glad to bring you an iced coffee, any flavor you choose. I'm just over at the Barks & Beans Cafe booth."

"Thank you, but I'm not really a coffee drinker." She looked at me more closely. "You must be Macy Hatfield. I recognize that red hair, like your brother's. It's good what you two are doing with that cafe, helping all those shelter dogs get adopted. Goodness knows we have too many strays around town."

My hair was more of a strawberry blonde, but I thanked her for her compliments and started walking her toward her tent. "I'm sorry you've had such a shock," I said.

"It really wasn't, though." She threw a dark look toward the joust ring. "I saw it coming in the cards."

I DROPPED Deanna off at her booth, then hurried over to grab her an iced water. August had been manning the fort alone, so a customer line had started to build.

Noting his distressed look, I said, "I'm sorry to leave you hanging. I'll be right back, so you can take your lunch break." He gave me a brief nod of acknowledgment, then busied himself with a coffee order.

The young redheaded fairy was sitting under Deanna's tent awning as I arrived. She seemed to be comforting Deanna, who was still crying in short bursts. I was relieved to see that the fairy seemed to have recovered from her earlier distress on the hill.

As I handed the water over, Deanna thanked me for everything and promised to visit our booth soon. Dabbing at her streaky cheeks with a tissue, she asked,

"Have you seen Eli or Cora around? I've been wondering where they went after Robbie's accident."

It wasn't exactly an accusation, but she'd obviously been thinking along the same lines as I had. Eli hadn't held back when he charged at Robbie. Although Doctor Stokes suspected an overdose, it was also possible that Eli had hit Robbie too hard, knocking him off the horse and causing him to get stomped.

"I haven't," I said.

She raised her penciled-in eyebrows, shooting a significant look at the topaz fairy. "I find that interesting."

The fairy nodded, but didn't respond. She seemed hesitant to join our conversation.

Sensing that she wanted to speak with Deanna more, I gave a quick wave. "Okay, well, just drop in if you need anything else."

A group of dwarves and elves strode past Deanna's tent, forcing me to wait until they'd passed. The dwarves' thick beards and the elves' long hair looked natural, as if they'd grown them for the occasion. Not to mention, their tailored costumes had elaborate embroidery details. These *Lord of the Rings* fans were certainly dedicated to their cosplay events.

Back at our cafe booth, the line had dwindled to one man who'd just gotten his coffee. I rang him up, then turned to August. "Thanks for keeping things running during that jousting accident. Could you see what happened from here?"

August ran a shaky hand through his black hair.

"Yeah, I did, and I couldn't believe it." He gave me an uneasy look. "Listen, I didn't get a chance to tell you earlier when Robbie came to our booth, but I actually know him."

"Personally?" Without waiting for his answer, I hurried to add, "I'm sorry you had to see him fall like that."

His eyes darkened. "Oh, it's not like we're friends. My dad is actually suing him."

I stayed quiet, because I didn't want to be rude and ask why. But August seemed to want to continue.

"The border of our cattle farm butts up against his property," he explained. "Robbie—Mr. Sears, I mean— is always moving his property marker back to give himself more land. Dad caught him doing it once, so he told him he'd better stop or he'd sue him. Mr. Sears just laughed and said he dared him to. Then Dad installed a hidden trail camera near the spot, and sure enough, Mr. Sears came back in the middle of the night and shifted the marker again. So my dad hired a lawyer, and he plans to take him to court over it. We need that land for our animals, Miss Hatfield."

"I understand," I said. And I did. Property disputes in West Virginia had to be taken seriously, because when tempers flared, someone might wind up drawing a weapon. I should know better than anyone how these feuds could blow up, given my Hatfield heritage.

"I feel bad that he fell off his horse, but in a way, I don't." His liquid-dark eyes met mine. "Is that wrong?"

Before I could give him an answer, Bo walked up,

clearly frustrated. He started peeling his knee socks off. "I can't wear these things one more minute. They must be made of wool."

He had sweat stains under his arms, and I could tell his blood pressure was up. He definitely embodied a stereotypical feisty redhead when he got irritated like this.

"Yes, they're wool," I said calmly. "That's part of your Highland garb, me lord."

"Maybe I'm not as Scottish as I thought," he said, then his face softened. "I'm sorry, sis." He turned to August. "I'm not usually so cranky, but this heat gets to me."

"I understand, Mister Hatfield." He glanced at his phone. "I'll probably head out on my lunch break now, if you don't mind?"

Bo hurried to assure him that he should take his time. Once August was out of earshot, I shared what he'd said about Robbie's land-grabbing ways.

"From what I can tell, Robbie is a regular piece of work," I said. "I saw him all over this fairground, hitting on every female he could. He even tried to flirt with me."

"I'm sure Titan loved that," Bo said grimly. He was probably imagining how he would've reacted if Robbie had hit on Summer.

It wouldn't have been pretty. While Titan tended to retreat and fall silent when things deeply bothered him, my brother was the exact opposite—he amped up the volume, making wide gestures and positioning himself even closer to the irritant.

"Where is Titan, by the way?" I asked. "I thought he was with you."

"He wanted me to tell you he'll be back soon. He had something he wanted to buy for his sisters before he headed back to the cabin."

It pleased me to see how genuinely Titan cared for his sisters, Cassandra and Ariadne. Apparently, Titan's mother had been obsessed with Greek lore long before the Percy Jackson books arrived on the scene, and she'd determined to give each of her children a myth-inspired name. Titan called his sisters Cass and Ari, respectively, and I had a feeling I was going to like them every bit as much as he did when we met, given all he'd told me about them.

Bo grinned. "You can't hide that smile on your face, sis. I'm glad Titan makes you so happy."

I blushed, looking out toward the main pathway. I caught a glimpse of Cora's red blouse as she and Eli walked past the glassblowing booth. They were walking hand in hand, as if they didn't have a care in the world.

I pointed her out to Bo. "That woman—Cora—is married to the knight who jousted Robbie, and she was threatening Robbie at our booth, basically saying her husband was going to clean his clock. It's strange how she sort of vanished after Robbie was knocked off his horse."

Bo looked thoughtful as he observed the couple

meandering along. Cora burst out laughing as the glassblower told some kind of joke.

While she certainly hadn't hidden her distaste for her ex, human decency seemed to demand that she show some measure of sadness over Robbie's terrible fall. In fact, Deanna's concern provided a stark contrast to Cora's nonchalance in regard to their ex.

"I find that very interesting," Bo said at last.

So did I.

4

The Sunday morning service ran a bit long, so by the time Titan and I settled into a booth at our favorite restaurant, I was salivating for some garlic breadsticks. As soon as the waitress brought the basket over, I dove right in.

By the time our entrees arrived, I realized I'd eaten three sticks to Titan's one, leaving a solitary breadstick behind. I hurried to apologize, but Titan didn't seem to mind in the least.

"You're welcome to have that one too, if you want," he said, reaching for the steak sauce. "This thick steak is going to fill me up fast."

He was a true gentleman, that one.

I took another bite of salad, then leaned in closer. "I've been wondering if Robbie's going to be okay, because I haven't heard any updates yet. Usually, Charlie keeps Bo in the loop on these kinds of things—especially if drugs were involved."

Charlie Hatcher was the detective in this area, and he was a close friend of ours. The fact that Bo was still able to use his DEA resources to help Charlie with local cases didn't hurt, either.

"I don't know," he mused. "Doctor Stokes thought it was an overdose, but the fact that Robbie bounced back without Narcan seems kind of strange." He added, "I should probably start carrying that stuff."

It was a sad commentary on the state of West Virginia that its law-abiding residents had to plan ahead and carry opioid antagonists so they'd be ready to help in case of a drug emergency. My thoughts flew to one of the primary facilitators of the drug trade in Lewisburg—Anne Louise Moreau, the woman who'd informed on her husband so he'd get thrown in prison, only to grab the reins of his crime empire. The FBI still hadn't apprehended her, despite their awareness that the petite blonde paid regular visits to her southern West Virginia domain.

I'd seen her once, so now I kept a constant eye out for her, because I wanted nothing more than to erase the scourge she'd brought into my hometown. Plus, she seemed to have some kind of warped obsession with my brother, even though she knew that Bo was relentless in his pursuit of justice. After all, he was the one who'd busted her husband.

As if sensing the dark direction of my thoughts, Titan asked, "You sure you want to head back to the faire tonight? You're not on duty, are you?"

I shook my head and swallowed my bite of salad.

"Milo will be working with Bo tonight, so I'm free to wander around, if I want. I was thinking of taking Coal along, since I got him that cute purple dragon costume. It makes him look a little like Toothless in the *How to Train Your Dragon* movie."

The waitress came over to ask if we wanted dessert, but I'd barely made it through half my chicken cacciatore, so I refused. Titan did the same.

Once she'd walked away, Titan asked, "Are you planning on digging into the Ren Faire dynamics, by any chance?"

I twirled pasta around my fork, then topped it with a piece of chicken. "I have to admit, it's a strange situation. Both Robbie's exes worked at the faire." After popping my bite into my mouth and savoring it, I said, "I've already talked with his first wife Deanna a little— she's the fortune-teller who goes by the name Crystal."

"Is she the one who was sobbing when Robbie fell?" He pounded on the bottom of the sauce bottle, only to produce a dime-sized amount for his final bites of steak.

"That's the one. She told me she'd foreseen that something bad was going to happen to him, but I don't believe in tarot cards. If anything, those readings put ideas in people's heads."

"I agree. My mom taught us to stay clear of that kind of thing," he said.

"Same." I took a hesitant bite of a pale, skinny green bean, but it wasn't nearly as tasty as the flat beans Auntie A liked to can. "Maybe Deanna wanted to scare him for some reason," I suggested. "But he didn't take her prophecy seriously, anyway. She said he basically laughed it off. That must've been what they were talking about when we passed him at her tent."

"He didn't seem the kind of guy to take anything seriously." His lips twisted in disapproval. He was probably thinking about Robbie's overly friendly manner with me and the other women on the fairground. "But I will say that he didn't strike me as being a drug user."

It wasn't outside the realm of possibility that when Robbie got knocked off his horse, the fall itself or that bone-breaking horse stomp had knocked him unconscious. Doc Stokes could've been wrong in his initial assessment, but in all these years, he'd never missed the mark in diagnosing my health issues, so I found that difficult to believe. If he suspected drugs, something along those lines was likely involved.

I was sure that Charlie would fill Bo in once they assessed Robbie's situation, and then Bo would tell me. I leaned back in my seat. "I'm stuffed," I said. "I'll get a box for my food, then we can hang out at home before we head to the faire."

Titan smiled. "I can't think of a better way to spend a Sunday afternoon."

THE AIR HAD COOLED off by the time we headed over to the faire, which was good, because Coal's purple dragon costume covered most of his torso. He didn't care for the hood, which featured big yellow eyeballs and horns, or for the spiked tail that sprang up from the rear of the outfit. Two small wings protruded from his sides, so maneuvering him into my compact SUV took some doing.

He managed to keep his whining to a minimum on our way over, possibly sensing he was about to have an adventure. Once I let him out in the parking lot and clipped his leash on, he was eager to go.

Titan had downsized his knightly garb, ditching the helmet and switching out the heavy metal for a simple chainmail vest. He wore a simple black tee under his vest, so his muscles were on full display, making it difficult for me to focus.

I'd tripped twice walking across a completely flat area.

I had tried to switch up my Viking dress by adding a cloth belt and a heavy silver necklace. But there'd been no need for me to make an effort—all eyes would be on Coal and Titan, anyway. How could anyone resist staring at a horse-sized dragon-dog and a dark-haired knight built like Superman?

We headed through the gates, waving toward Bo and Milo before veering off in the other direction. We wanted to take in some sights before circling back to the cafe booth.

Bright flags fluttered atop poles circling the jousting arena, providing a cheery contrast to the accident that had occurred just yesterday. As we passed a booth where fox and coyote pelts flapped in the breeze,

Coal gave a sudden, deep *woof*. The owner almost jumped out of her skin, stumbling against a table loaded with hide rugs. I told Coal to sit down, trying to explain that he'd simply been startled by her furs.

The woman edged a bit closer, giving him a tentative smile. "He's a regular Scooby-Doo, isn't he?"

Sensing that he'd been out of line, Coal arranged his lips into something resembling a friendly smile. But when he stood up, his upright dragon tail poked into a stand of fur bags, knocking it to the ground. Titan hurriedly set the stand upright, but I pulled Coal's leash tight so we could beat a hasty exit.

Titan caught up with us near the castle maze and gave Coal a light pat on the back. "Poor boy. You were just trying to be friendly, weren't you?"

"It might've been a mistake to bring him," I said. "I usually have him wear his muzzle when we're out, because I know how scary it can be for him to bark and show his teeth to strangers. They don't understand that he's more scared than aggressive."

Titan shrugged. "It's okay. His hood kind of wraps his jaw, so he can't even do a full-fledged bark. He's clearly under control."

Noticing two small children pointing at Coal and smiling, I let out a breath. "You're right. People can tell he means well, and it's not like he's tearing around chasing people." Taking a closer look at the castle maze, I said, "I've always wanted to do that—test my puzzle-solving skills and all."

He grinned. "You want to try it now?"

"Sure." I walked Coal toward the attendant, but she took a step back, shaking her head. "No dogs allowed in the maze," she said hoarsely, pointing at Coal. Her black witch costume seemed to match her dark mood.

"Oh, of course." I stepped backward, making way for the next child in line.

But Titan was having none of it. "Here, give me his leash," he said. "You do the maze and try your skills. Coal and I will be waiting for you at the exit."

The surly attendant none-too-gently stamped my hand so I could enter. "There's only one way out," she said, her black lips flattening into a smirk. "All you have to do is find it."

I opened the wooden door and walked in, glancing around at the gray stone-like walls. The path veered off in a couple of directions, so I chose the one on the right. With each new turn, I took the right path, figuring sooner or later I'd get out.

But it didn't take long before the walls all started to look the same. I couldn't find any distinctive marks anywhere, and since the top was enclosed, I couldn't use the sky to orient myself. I heard children giggling up ahead, but couldn't tell how to reach them. Every turn I made led me into short, empty tunnels that didn't seem to be leading me toward the exit.

Sweat beaded on my lip, and I started to feel claustrophobic. I'd gotten completely turned around and had no idea which direction was which. I felt like a fool —why had I wanted to do a child's maze, anyway?

Even more concerning—how did those poor children find their way out of here? If I'd been a child ramming through this morass, I would have definitely burst into tears.

I felt like doing that now. What was wrong with me?

Forcing myself to take another turn, I startled to see a hideous plague doctor standing at the end of the path, staring at me with beady red eyes. The beak-masked person didn't say one word, instead shifting broad shoulders under a black cape.

I finally found my voice and said, "Excuse me. I'm trying to find my way to the exit."

Instead of pointing me in a direction, the ominous plague doctor cackled and rushed directly toward me. I instinctively closed my eyes and folded into myself, stepping back as the person's black cape swished by, brushing against my arms. Surely they wouldn't dare attack me in the middle of the fairground?

But when I opened my eyes, the terror was nowhere in sight.

What kind of a sick joke was that? Had the faire actually hired someone to stand inside the maze and scare people? That would hardly seem funny to the kids walking through.

I heaved a sigh, trying to figure out if I should move forward or attempt to retrace my steps. Just then, I heard a gentle bark coming from somewhere on my left. It was undoubtedly Coal.

Had he somehow understood that I was in trouble? Maybe he was giving me a clue—like any good Scooby-

Doo doggie—and letting me know which way the exit was.

Relief poured through me, and I forced myself to focus. There was low black scuff mark on the wall in front of me. Some kid had probably gotten fed up with hunting for a way out and given it a kick.

It turned out to be a helpful act of vandalism. I was able to use the scuff as a sort of home base, moving toward the direction of the bark. Slowly but surely, one careful turn after another, the exit door came into view.

I careened out of it straight toward Titan, who was waiting off to one side. Coal pressed his body against my leg, shoving his dragon hood under my hand for a comforting pat. I was only too happy to oblige.

"What happened?" Titan asked. "I was getting worried. Coal got anxious, too—he was panting, then he barked at nothing in particular."

"I think he knew I was confused," I explained. "I got all turned around, but his bark let me know where you were. And just at the right time, too—I ran into some weird person in a plague doctor costume. Did you see someone like that come out?"

Titan shook his head. "Only a couple of kids and their mom."

I gave the offensive labyrinth one last look. "Well, I sure won't be going in there again, believe you me." Glancing up toward the fairy forest, I noticed a man shooting a bow and arrow. "Let's go blow off some steam, shall we?"

5

W hile I didn't have much of a naturally competitive bent, Titan surely did, and he was only too happy to defeat anyone and everyone who challenged him at the archery booth. This included the booth owner, who had innocently dared Titan into a competition involving trick shots through rings hung in the trees.

By the time Titan was finished, a crowd had gathered to cheer for him, as if his superior shots would somehow save the people of the land, like Robin Hood.

I patted him on the back as he chose rewards for each victory, practically cleaning the booth out. When he opened a small ring box to reveal a plastic gemstone ring, he offered it to me with a flourish. "For my lady," he said.

The lingering bystanders swooned, and for a moment, I debated slipping the ring on my engagement finger. But I didn't want to jump the gun—especially since I wasn't quite ready for marriage, and I didn't want to lead Titan on. I slipped it onto my opposite finger, giving him a hug instead.

He looked disappointed, but soon rallied. "Let's check out the next booth," he suggested. "I read about it in the faire brochure—the lady there makes jewelry from animal bones."

A long-buried fact rose to the surface. "Our mom was part Inuit," I mused. "I wonder if they have anything made with walrus tusks, or maybe reindeer antler."

Titan slowed, giving me a tender look. He knew I rarely talked about my parents, since they'd both died in a sudden creek flood when Bo and I were young. The deep compassion in his gaze spoke louder than any words could.

He tucked his strong arm under mine, walking Coal and me toward the booth. "If you see anything you like, I want to get it for you. Just say the word."

I swallowed at the lump in my throat, knowing that with Titan, all I ever had to do was say the word.

THE BONE CARVER was deep into explaining her process to us when I caught a glimpse of a short, armored knight hurrying down the path. There were so few fully armored knights around, I guessed that it might be the same person Robbie had handed his green water bottle off to before mounting his horse.

It seemed like a good chance to find out the knight's identity. After all, he should have stepped up and spoken to the police when they'd showed up on the fairground, since he was the last person to interact with Robbie. Yet he hadn't been around since the start of the joust.

Had he been hiding?

Handing Coal's leash over to Titan, I whispered, "I'll be right back. I just want to catch up with that knight." He gave me a curious look, but returned his focus to the necklace the woman had removed from its case to show him.

I jogged up behind the knight, noticing a large tattoo of a male lion on the back of his hand. But the moment he turned around and realized I was coming up on him, he took off running. He was surprisingly nimble for someone in a full suit of armor. I felt even more convinced he might have something to hide.

He hurried past the bench seating for the outdoor theater, then ducked behind the stage. I stepped toward the benches, only to catch him slipping under the roped-off area into the back woods.

Before I could chase him, a black blur emerged from the side of the theater and shifted into my path.

It was the loathsome plague doctor. He held up a gloved hand, revealing nasty black claws on his fingertips. Although he didn't speak a word, his message came through loud and clear—I wasn't to follow the knight.

What was going on here? I didn't take kindly to

being bullied on a public fairground—or anywhere, for that matter.

I stood my ground. "Who are you?" I demanded.

Titan's concerned shout rang out behind me. "Macy, you okay?"

Footsteps thudded my way, and I knew Coal was probably close on Titan's heels.

I turned and waved. "I'm fine," I said.

But by the time I turned back toward the plague doctor, he had disappeared. Titan reached my side, with Coal struggling to catch up in his unwieldy costume. My Dane's tongue lolled out, leaving no doubt he needed water—and soon.

I sighed. "I lost both of them." Taking Coal's leash, I walked over and sat down, so he could take a breather.

"Who were you trying to catch?" Titan asked.

"I saw that knight who was with Robbie just before the joust—at least, I'm pretty sure it was him, since he ran from me like he had something to hide." I shook my head. "Then that stinking plague doctor showed up and blocked my path. I'm starting to think he's following me around. Anyway, I'm sure there's no catching up with the knight now, but I noticed a distinctive tattoo on his hand. It was of a thick-maned lion."

Titan nodded. "Good work—that's a start at finding him." He hesitantly pulled a box from his pocket and opened it, revealing a stunning carved-bone necklace on a gold chain. "It's made from reindeer antler, she said— also known as caribou in North America. I thought you

deserved something better than the plastic ring I won."
As he extended the necklace box toward me, Coal's eyes
brightened, as if sensing that Titan wished to please me.

"It's beautiful." I touched the cool ivory-colored
pendant, unable to put into words how much his gift
meant. It honored a piece of my mother's heritage,
which was something Auntie A had told me she'd held
dear.

"We'd better get Coal some water," I said. "Let's
head back to the Barks & Beans booth and pick some
up. I can tell Bo to keep an eye out for that short
knight. And Detective Hatcher should know about
him, too."

"I agree." He placed both hands on my shoulders,
and his eyes flashed protectively. "Next time, wait for
me to catch up. I don't want you getting hurt."

Titan was not the type to make off-the-cuff
remarks. He felt things deeply, and he also took the
time to think before saying anything. So even as he
said he didn't want me getting hurt, his eyes and his
firm grip were telling me the rest of the story—that
he'd destroy anyone who dared to lay a wayward hand
upon me.

It felt like a strange shift of power. Up until now, my
brother had been my primary protector (after Auntie
A, who would've fought tooth and nail for us). He'd
always come running to take on any threats that
entered my life, which included the most unexpected
one—my ex, Jake.

Even though Bo and Jake hadn't had a face-to-face encounter since my divorce, I was hoping it stayed that way. Bo wasn't the type who would let that particular sleeping dog lie. Jake had cheated and then left me, and in Bo's book, that level of betrayal was practically unforgiveable.

But Titan was letting me know he was more than prepared to step into Bo's role. He wanted to, in fact. And I couldn't sort through all the feelings that brought to the surface. It was like starting over outside the umbrella of my brother's watchful care. I had no doubt that Titan was up to the task, but to trust him, I had to believe he would never give up on me...and that was difficult, after Jake.

I finally managed to give him a reassuring nod, then silently led Coal toward the path. Titan fell into step behind me, his presence as strong as a physical shield.

No knights or plague doctors would be sneaking up on me anytime soon.

SUMMER WAS SITTING on a bench as we approached the booth, and when she stood, I literally stopped short to stare. She was dressed as Galadriel from *The Lord of the Rings*, in an all-white dress that hinted at how she would look as a bride. Her honey-colored waves spilled below her silver headpiece, and although she wore no makeup, she looked more regal than any queen I'd ever seen.

I hurried over to give her a hug. "You look absolutely spellbinding! Magical!"

She grinned. "That was the overall intent." Inching her hem up a little, she showed off the white boots she'd told me she found on clearance. "Plus, I can walk around comfortably. You can't beat that!"

I stole a glance at Bo. Even as he was handing a bag to a customer, he kept glancing Summer's way, as if to verify that she was real. His wide-eyed look spoke volumes about his feelings toward his fiancée. He clearly couldn't get enough of her.

Summer headed back to finish her iced drink, so I walked over to grab a dish and some water for Coal. With the customers cleared out, Titan and Bo had started talking.

Milo called out a *hello* to me, and I had to do a double-take. He'd been growing out his blond hair for a few months, and today he'd let his longer bangs tumble over one eye. His face looked dirty, like he'd smudged it, and he was sporting a rough-spun linen shirt and dark pants. He gave me a winsome smirk, and I realized exactly who he was—the "Farm Boy" Westley, from *The Princess Bride*.

What a perfectly ironic outfit for the upper-crust guy who came to work simply because he enjoyed it, and not because he had any need of the income.

"Hand me a couple of water bottles, Farm Boy," I joked.

"You recognized me," he said. "Can you believe that you're the first person to do that today?" As he handed the water bottles over, he said, "As you wish."

"I'll also need that blue bowl behind the counter," I added.

Somewhat less enthusiastically, he passed me the large dog bowl I'd stashed for Coal. As I poured the bottles into it, Coal started lapping up the water. I caught a movement out of the corner of my eye and stood.

Charlie Hatcher was stalking straight toward the counter. The serious look on his face told me that something unpleasant must have happened.

When Bo saw him, he fell silent, and so did Titan. We all stared, knowing the detective wouldn't have dropped in unannounced for no reason.

Skipping the pleasantries, he said, "Robbie Sears passed away this morning, and we have a problem. He didn't die of an overdose. His tox screen showed he was poisoned."

6

W e stood in stunned silence for a moment, letting the news sink in.

"Poisoned?" Bo repeated. "With what? Doctor Stokes told me Robbie had respiratory depression. I thought that generally corresponds with an opioid overdose."

"It often does. But this time it wasn't showing opioids, so Doctor Stokes suggested running a secondary, specialized tox screen. That one showed that he was overdosed with another drug—it's one I have a little trouble pronouncing." Charlie glanced at the black notepad in his hand. "It's Tetra-hydro-zoline," he sounded out. "Which happens to be eye drops. He couldn't have accidentally ingested the heavy dose that was in his system, so this is now a homicide investigation."

Titan's eyes widened. "You're saying he somehow *ate* eye drops?"

Summer stood up and edged closer, but the detective didn't seem to mind. She was in our inner circle, so she'd find out what was going on one way or another.

The disarming dimple in Charlie's cheek all but disappeared as he frowned. "I'm saying someone deliberately administered them into his food or drink, and in a large quantity." He glanced around. "That's what brings me here today. He was last seen drinking from a Barks & Beans Cafe cup."

Bo started shaking his head. "Wait—you know we had nothing to do with this, Charlie."

The detective met his gaze. "I'm just gathering information right now, Bo. You know it's nothing personal. I figured one of you might have some insight into Robbie's movements yesterday, since he stopped in for a drink."

I thought back to Robbie's visit. "He was eating a kielbasa when he came over. We served him an iced chai latte, but that was at least an hour before his joust. You might want to check with the stand that sells kielbasas. But if he'd been poisoned then, it seems like he would've been showing side effects long before his joust."

"I would think so, but I'll have to ask the doctor how long that kind of dose would take to kick in." Charlie scrawled something in his notepad. "Did he finish his drink here, maybe dump his cup in the trash?"

I shook my head. "He took it over to Cosmic Crystal's booth—we saw him talking with her soon after.

Her real name is Deanna, and she's actually one of his ex-wives."

The detective raised one steely gray eyebrow, but kept writing.

Titan added, "He was also approaching several other women while we were walking around on lunch break." His tone was laced with disapproval.

"With 'approaching' being the key word," I explained. "The women didn't seem pleased by his advances."

Charlie gave me a knowing nod. "So, you last saw him holding your cup at Deanna's tent?"

"Yes. She was clearly upset about something, but Charlie seemed to be laughing at her. She told me later that she'd warned him that her cards had predicted he was in danger, but he didn't take her seriously."

"Could that have been some kind of cover for her to kill him herself?" he asked.

I contemplated that possibility. "It wouldn't make sense for her to try to warn him before poisoning him. Besides, she seemed really devastated when he fell off the horse. She was one of the first to run over, and she couldn't stop crying afterward. I think she genuinely cared about him." I hesitated. "Meanwhile, his other ex, Cora, vanished from the field once Robbie fell. So did her husband, Eli—the one who knocked Robbie off his horse."

"I see," Charlie observed.

"Wait a minute," I added. "That latte wasn't the last thing Robbie drank. I saw him drinking out of a green water bottle just before the joust. He handed it off to a shorter knight, who then helped him mount his horse."

"Robbie did seem a bit tottery on his saddle as he rode into the ring," Titan added thoughtfully. "I noticed he wasn't holding his lance properly. You'd think he would, given that he'd practiced the act before."

"And we just saw that knight by the outdoor theater," I said. "I tried to catch up with him to encourage him to talk with the police about Robbie's final moments, but he ran from me."

Concern shot across Bo's face. Titan caught his look and took a step closer to me. "It did seem suspicious," he said.

Milo suddenly butted in. "Who served Robbie his chai latte?"

I was confused as to why Milo would inject himself into our conversation, since he hadn't been working yesterday. "August did," I said. "Why?"

"I've heard his dad was involved in a lawsuit against his neighbor, who happens to be Robbie Sears. It just seemed odd to me, because last week, I overheard August talking with Bristol about untraceable poisons."

I couldn't believe Milo was throwing this suggestion out there. Rushing to August's defense, I said, "He's studying to become a forensic investigator. Of course he's going to be reading about different methods of poisoning."

Charlie seemed thoughtful. "This is the Blackwell boy? I know his dad, Owen. He's been farming that land for years. He's very attached to it—stayed there even after his wife died young, from cancer. I've heard tell of him getting into it with a neighbor at the corner diner—that must've been Robbie."

Milo was looking rather pleased with himself, which I found exasperating. Why was he attacking our new employee?

Charlie turned to me. "Did you actually watch August making the latte?"

I couldn't believe he was going down this rabbit trail, but I had to give him an honest answer. "Well, not exactly. I mean, he had to turn around to get the milk from the fridge." I glanced at Bo, wishing he would chime in, but he probably hadn't been watching August make the latte. And Titan had stayed focused on Robbie. "He's been a conscientious employee, and I'm sure he wouldn't have jeopardized his education to poison his neighbor," I blurted out.

Charlie's face was completely neutral, giving away none of his suspicions. "Thanks—this has been really helpful. I'll be following up on things. You all know where to reach me if anything new turns up, or if you happen to find out who that knight is." He fixed me with a fatherly look. "But don't go bombing around looking for him, Macy. You might get more than you bargained for, if he does turn out to be our poisoner. I can ask around, try to find out which knight was on duty to help him onto the horse yesterday."

He gave a polite dip of his head, then strode off in the direction of Cosmic Crystal's tent.

Once he was out of sight, I turned toward Milo and

demanded, "Why would you try to throw August under the bus like that? You're acting more like the Dread Pirate Roberts than Westley."

Milo shoved his bangs to the side, exposing wide, innocent blue eyes. "I thought you'd want me to tell the truth."

That was hardly the entire story, but before I could probe further, Coal gave a soft whine at my side. He was ready to go home, and as it turned out, so was I.

"Maybe we should head back," I said. "Coal's done with his costume."

Titan nodded his agreement, so I stepped over to give Bo and Summer quick hugs, then managed a curt "Goodbye" for Milo. I planned to talk with him this week about his animosity toward August, because we couldn't have our Barks & Beans employees attacking one another.

As we made our way into the parking lot, Titan said, "I can't believe Robbie died—and from eye drops, no less. Who would think of using something like that?"

"Someone familiar with poisons. And, whether I like it or not, August fits that bill," I admitted. "I didn't catch his conversation with Bristol about poison methods, but he did mention checking out a book on the Medici family to me the other day. I suppose he could have some sort of weird fascination with the subject."

"But even if he did, why would he risk squeezing eye drops into the drink *he* served Robbie? Seems like he would've guessed that something like that would get him caught."

I halted next to my SUV so I could ease Coal's dragon hood off. He melted me with a grateful look, then wagged his tail. Titan was unfortunately standing right next to him, so he got whapped in the shin.

"Whoa, there, boy," Titan said. "How about we take off the rest of that costume?"

We worked together to strip Coal of his dragon gear, which allowed him to climb into the back of the vehicle unaided. Titan opened the driver's side door to let me in, then he headed around to the passenger's side. Once he'd buckled up, he asked, "Am I wrong in thinking that Milo and Bristol are an item now?"

I drove toward the long, dusty driveway. "Yes, they do a lot together, but I'm not sure if he's officially asked her to be his girlfriend yet," I said.

"I'm wondering if that might be part of his issue. Didn't you say that Bristol had recommended August for the job?"

I nodded. "They grew up together. I think August plays video games with Bristol's brother or something."

"But August is around Bristol's age, right? And he's so different from Milo. As an introvert myself, I'm guessing that August is one, too. That seems like the direct opposite of Milo, who's always outgoing. What if our friendly neighborhood barista is a little jealous over Bristol's relationship with this dark and brooding newbie?"

There it was, as clear as the nose on my face. He

was right, of course. Milo had seen an opportunity to make August look bad, and he'd pounced on it.

"Thanks for spelling that out for me," I said. "I can't believe I missed Milo's green-with-envy vibes."

"I know a little something about twenty-something dudes," he said modestly. "Sometimes those dark horse introverts swoop in and get the girl." The corner of his lips twisted up in a wry grin. "We're kind of dangerous that way."

"Oh, I can believe it." I gave his hand a squeeze. "And I'm so glad you are."

7

Milo and August were both scheduled to work Monday, and so was I, so I determined to monitor their interactions to see if Titan was right about Milo's envy of August.

The day started out fairly low-key, with Summer dropping off two black dogs named Shawn and Henry Spencer, respectively. Hilariously, even though Shawn was taller and Henry had a shorter coat length, they somehow resembled a son and father, just like their namesakes on the *Psych* TV show. Lassiter the hound had already been adopted, and I was guessing that was largely due to his name and dejected look.

Milo kept busy at the Beans counter, whipping up coffee drinks and chatting with Jimmy, our retired high school bus driver barista, while I continued to train August in the Barks section. He was good with dogs, as he'd told us, but he had to work on his people skills so he could put customers at ease with the shelter animals.

Today, August was looking particularly retro with a black Depeche Mode T-shirt he might've picked up at a Goodwill. His jeans were wide-legged and baggy, and he wore beat-up Adidas tennies. I wasn't sure if he was making some kind of style statement or just wearing his everyday attire.

Yet there was something deep and solid about August. It was easy to engage him in conversation, and each time I did, his love for learning shone through. I asked about his forensics program, and he was eager to tell me about it. Arson was the current topic in his Forensic Science class, and he had some crazy stories to share.

He was bringing Henry and Shawn in from their bathroom walk when Milo opened the low doggie gate and strode into the Barks section. He gave August a pointed look as he spoke.

"We have a customer who complained about the dogs barking in the fenced yard while she was trying to enjoy her tea by the window. She said she couldn't even hear herself think. I see that you had them outside? Is there some way you could rein them in, or is that beyond your capabilities?"

August gave no response, instead stroking the dogs' black fur. He seemed bored by the verbal attack, which probably enraged Milo even more.

"Milo," I scolded. "They would've been barking just

as much if I'd taken them out. You can't keep dogs from getting excited." I glanced into the Beans section.

It took me about one second to determine the actual source of the complaint. Her head was turned toward the window, but her frizzy gray hair and over-sized, thick glasses gave her away. Not to mention her granny-style cardigan and the cane propped against her table.

I lowered my voice and stepped in closer to Milo. "You're seriously reporting a complaint from Matilda Crump? She gripes around each and every time she comes into the cafe—in fact, it might be her favorite pastime. I'd wager she complained about the tea you gave her, too. A bit watery? Or maybe too cold? Am I right?"

Milo haughtily cleared his throat. "That's beside the point. The point is that August seems to be having trouble keeping the shelter dogs in check, and that's a large part of his job."

August gave a slow blink, as if trying to make sense of what Milo was saying.

I took Milo's arm and steered him toward the dog gate. "I appreciate your warning about the dogs, but would you have done the same thing if Bristol had been the one walking them?"

Milo stiffened at the mention of Bristol's name. "I assumed it was expected of me to report customer complaints, Miss Hatfield."

The fact that he was throwing in my boss title

didn't impress me. "You're assuming a lot these days, Milo," I said quietly. "I'll deal with Matilda."

Alarm shot across his face, but he tossed his bangs to the side and stalked back to the coffee bar.

I walked over to Matilda, who was sipping on her tea and crumbling pieces off her scone. She gave me a cursory nod and said, "Lovely day, isn't it? I decided to take a stroll and pick up one of Charity's scrummy almond scones." She dropped another crumble to her napkin. "But it's a smidge dry, I have to say."

No, she didn't *have* to say. I'd give her the benefit of the doubt, though, and assume that "scrummy" was short for "scrumptious" instead of a cloaked way of saying "crummy." Matilda liked to use an affected British accent and phraseology, even though she'd been born and reared in the U.S. of A.

My jaw felt tight. "I'm sorry our scones—and our dogs—aren't up to your expectations. Perhaps Milo could give you another pastry to go. It'll be on the house." Maybe she'd pick up on my not-so-subtle hint that she leave.

She peered at me through her thick lenses. "Why, I wouldn't think of taking advantage. I pay my own way, young lady. I know your generation is used to having things handed to them for free, but not mine. Like my dear husband always used to say—"

"I'm afraid I have to get back to my dogs." I didn't want to get sucked down Matilda's rabbit hole of unsolicited advice, since it never seemed to have a stopping point.

She'd slighted my entire generation—although she probably had no idea which generation I was part of—and now seemed blissfully unaware of her thinly veiled insult.

"Of course." She patted my hand. "Have a brilliant day, my dear."

What a Monday. I'd gone from negotiating a senseless attack from Milo to fielding an equally senseless attack from Matilda. Unlike my brother, I preferred peace to fighting. Bo was only too happy to wade into a battle and—not surprisingly—end it.

Although I couldn't say the same for Matilda, Milo wasn't a troublemaker by nature. If we wanted to keep the cafe waters calm, we were going to have to negotiate some kind of truce between Milo and August.

I hated to bother Bo on his day off, but I sat down in the dog section and shot him a quick text. "Milo and August having issues. Let's talk tonight since it's just me. I'll bring sweet tea."

I'd just invited myself over to Bo's house, but I knew that he'd only be too happy to make supper for two. He enjoyed feeding me, since he knew that I tended to live off frozen foods, accompanied with the occasional rice or pasta.

And tonight Titan was hanging out with his FBI friend Julius, who somehow reminded me of Julius Caesar with his sharp eyes, close-cropped hair, and powerful persona. I'd have plenty of time to discuss cafe matters with my brother.

Bo's text came back quickly. "Come over at 7. I'm

making chicken enchiladas, so I'll have plenty for both of us and leftovers for Titan."

I agreed, then tucked my phone in my back pocket. August gave me a curious look, as if wondering if everything was okay.

I smiled. "There's nothing you could've done differently. Don't worry about it. You're doing a fine job here."

August threw a chew toy to Shawn, who attacked it with gusto. "Milo informed me that Robbie Sears died. I had no idea. That's awful. I would've helped with his CPR, but I don't get trained in that until my last semester."

So Milo had tried to guilt-trip August, as well. He was like a little whirlwind of jealousy, wreaking all the damage he could possibly inflict.

"Robbie was given CPR by professionals, so there's nothing to feel bad about," I said. "Unfortunately, it was probably too late anyway. I suppose Milo also told you Robbie was poisoned?"

August gave a slow nod. "I think Milo got the idea I have some kind of grudge against Robbie. It's true that I didn't care for the man—he was trying to steal land from my dad—but I never would've harmed him."

"Of course you wouldn't have," I said. "Don't let Milo get under your skin."

His dark eyes met and held mine. "I don't really take him seriously."

Wow, what a burn. Had August shared his dismissive thoughts about Bristol's almost-boyfriend with her? Was it possible he cared for Bristol himself? Maybe Milo was picking up on some actual romantic undercurrents.

A love triangle at the cafe could never turn out well. Bo and I needed to get this rivalry in hand, and as quickly as possible.

I PLUNGED a huge bite of enchilada into ranch dip, then savored the spicy/cool combination on my tongue. "These are perfect, as usual," I said.

Bo took a sip of sweet tea—one of the only things I could make well. "So you're telling me we need to do damage control between those boys. Any ideas on how to go about that?"

"We could make them sit down and talk it out," I suggested.

He frowned. "That might not work so well with guys—especially young guys." He leaned back in his chair. "Let me tell you a little story. Back in the DEA, we had two operatives who were always hostile toward each other, because their personalities didn't line up. They couldn't even share the same quarters. But then they did a door breach exercise together, and it turned out their explosive was faulty. One of the guys lost two fingers on the spot. Without hesitation, the other guy wrapped his hand and sat with him until help came. After that, they reached some kind of understanding.

They were able to tolerate and even joke with one another."

I swirled the ice in my tea. "So what you're saying is that we need to blow something up?"

"Very funny. I'm saying we need to get them working together toward some common goal. It might be painful, but it needs to happen."

Shooting him a defiant look, I said, "So help me, if you suggest falling backward into our colleagues' arms, I'm out. I trust no one that much."

He chuckled. "Me, neither." After thinking for a moment, he added, "Hey, didn't you say Milo wanted to learn to do coffee foam art like Kylie? What if we had her train both of them on it—together?"

I considered his suggestion. Outside of Bo, Kylie was the one person in the cafe who might be scary enough to demand the rivals cooperate. Between her tattoos, her combat boots, and her tough-as-nails attitude, no one would dare cross her.

"Excellent idea, bro. I'll talk with Kylie and try to set something up this week, maybe after work hours."

"Good." He sighed. "Listen, you know things are getting bad when Charity complains about Milo's irritability of late. She actually told me she wished she could—and I quote—'crack a can of whoop-butt' on him."

I practically spat out my tea. "Charity comes off all soft, like the pastries she bakes, but I think she has a backbone of steel. Remember how she threatened that drug dealer Boss Hogg with a baseball bat, telling him to leave her son alone? I still can't get over that story."

Bo stood, sweeping Stormy into his arms and rubbing her behind the ears. Her rattling purr cranked up to full volume. "You know how it is, sis. When it comes to family, no holds are barred."

That was certainly the case for us Hatfields. But it made me wonder if August had felt the same way toward his father's nemesis. Surely he wouldn't have resorted to drastic measures to end a bitter land dispute, but it wouldn't be the first time something like that had happened.

8

Once Coal had snuggled up on his pillow at the foot of my bed, I climbed under my quilt and scrolled through the local news. I wanted to see if they'd reported anything on Robbie's untimely death.

To my surprise, the reporter was interviewing a woman named Rosetta Blackwell, who turned out to be the head of a local women's shelter called Rosie's Refuge. The tall, silver-haired woman sat in a floral upholstered chair, explaining that she'd been inspired to open the shelter due to her own personal experience.

"I was married to an abusive man," she said quietly. "Then I finally gathered up my courage and fled that marriage. I brought my son, Owen, to this area, since I grew up here. I decided to convert my home into a women's shelter to help other women and children get on their feet, like we did."

The reporter asked her how many employees she

had, and she said, "My son Owen and my grandson help maintain the house and grounds. We also receive donations from generous clubs and organizations, so we are never at a lack for resources."

So Owen Blackwell and his son spent their free time—what little of it there probably was—helping out with Rosie's Refuge. That made me feel all the more endeared toward August. He was a good kid, and I didn't care what Milo said about him.

My text tone pinged, so I scrambled to switch to that screen, wondering if Titan had forgotten to tell me something. When we'd talked earlier, he told me that the FBI wanted him to follow up on some things in the area, which would keep him busy during my work days. But we planned to get together for as many meals as we could, then hang out at the faire on the weekend.

The text had come from Kylie, though. She was agreeing to the impromptu session on foam art design. "Let's shoot for Thursday night after work, if Milo and August can clear some time. And yeah, I'm getting sick of this weird dynamic between them. They have to get things resolved."

I agreed, then sent out texts to see if the guys could make it. In the meantime, I planned on asking August some questions about his grandma's shelter. I wanted to support a place where women could get away from their bad husbands...after all, that's basically why Bo created the Barks & Beans Cafe. It was to help me achieve my deepest dreams after my husband left me. I would never be able to thank him enough for that fresh start—and for being the one to introduce me to Titan.

AFTER A QUICK SUPPER THURSDAY NIGHT, I headed into the cafe via the connecting door from my house. I turned on some lights and unlocked the main door, making sure the outside sign stayed flipped to *Closed*. I didn't want any curious passersby dropping in, hoping for an evening coffee fix.

Kylie was the first to arrive, wearing black jeans and a black tank top. Her new pixie cut showed off the dragon tattoo running up her neck, and her standard black boots thudded as she walked. She looked intimidating as all get-out, and the look in her hazel eyes said she was all business.

She hustled around, turning on machines and setting supplies on the counter. "You staying here?" she asked. "It'll only take half an hour or so, then you can lock up behind us." She winked. "I promise to make you a kickin' decaf gingerbread latte."

She knew my weakness. We didn't start making gingerbread lattes until December, but they were one of my all-time favorite coffee drinks. Besides, it wouldn't hurt to hang out and see how things went between our quarrelsome young employees.

"Sure, I'll stay." I settled into a comfy white chair. "But if those two get going with each other—"

Her eyes flashed. "I'll shut them down. I'm not

staying here all night, believe me. They're going to work this thing out and learn how to do foam art in the process."

Clearly, Kylie understood her mission. I gave her an encouraging nod as the door opened and August walked in. He seemed a bit subdued—tired, maybe?—and he'd grown a stubble beard since yesterday. It made him look a little older. After giving both of us a friendly greeting, he headed behind the counter to help Kylie.

Milo was the next to arrive. Although his lips were tight and he appeared tense, he managed to shoot me a smile and a friendly, "Evening, Miss Hatfield." He was nothing if not Southern gentry.

Before long, Kylie had them taking turns brewing up lattes. She interjected a few tips as they went through the process, and both seemed ready to accept her suggestions.

But then Milo decided it was time to attack.

"What kind of a name is 'August,' anyway?" He smirked. "I think I'll call you 'Auguste.' It'll give you a little more flair."

Kylie glanced over, catching my watchful eye.

August shrugged, frothing the milk for his latte. "It means great or magnificent in Latin." Without even looking at Milo, he casually continued, "Now, am I right in thinking that the name 'Milo' comes from a flower?"

Milo flushed, suddenly focusing on his foam art. Then, seeming to think better of his retreat, he jutted his chin out toward August. "Your dad is always stirring up trouble," he said. "You know he got banned from the Town of Lewisburg Facebook page when he started posting how the pipeline would mess up all the groundwater."

August calmly set his latte art tool down and turned, so he was facing Milo head-on. He was totally in control, which made him seem all the more threatening. "He was sharing the truth. Sediment from the blasting contaminates wells—wells that farmers like my dad use to feed animals." His dark eyes flashed. "But you wouldn't care about that. You and your ilk only care about the big money businesses, like the pipeline. Not the little people who supply grass-fed beef to your fancy restaurants."

Kylie held up a hand. "Boys, *boys*. Your boss is sitting *right there*." She gestured in my direction. "And nothing's stopping her from firing both of you on the spot. I think I would. You need to drop this petty stuff and get a life. You're not teenagers anymore."

Duly chastened, the guys returned their attention to their lattes. In a few moments, Kylie walked my way. She handed me a gingerbread latte with a foam-art Great Dane on top.

"As promised." She shot me a rueful grin. "Sorry that took so long."

"No problem. It looks great." I wrapped the mug in my hands, allowing it to warm my chilly fingers.

"I'm hoping lessons have been learned tonight," she whispered.

"I think so," I whispered back.

Milo finished his foam art, then brought the mug over to show me the finished design, which was a large dog bone.

I gave him an encouraging smile. "You're getting into the true spirit of the Barks & Beans Cafe, I see."

He beamed back at me, and it hit me that praise was important to our proud barista. It was entirely possible that his parents—who were rarely home, from what I could tell—didn't compliment him often. Plus, I'd gotten the impression that his older brother Hudson tended to steal his thunder.

Milo drank his latte, then pointedly ignored August as he walked over to wash his mug. Once he'd told me goodnight and thanked Kylie for the lesson, he headed out.

August was still taking his time. Even as Kylie cleaned, he stayed focused on his task.

Once she was finished, she glanced into his mug. "That's amazing work," she said. "Are you getting done anytime soon, though? I need to get home."

He raised his head and gave her a blank look, like he'd been lost in a dream. "Oh, sure. I just wanted to get this right."

"A rose by any other name..." Kylie said. She turned to me. "You need to check this out."

I walked over and looked at August's art. He'd designed a detailed, full-petaled rose. "That's beautiful," I murmured. "Isn't your grandmother named Rosetta? I saw her on the news."

He nodded. "I tend to the rosebushes at her shelter. She has some rare heirloom breeds."

It was the opening I'd needed. "I wondered if I could drop by and visit sometime, but I wasn't sure where it was located. I'd like to support her shelter somehow."

"They don't list the address publicly, for the safety of the residents," August explained. "But I can give you the location. I know Gran would like to meet you. She was excited to hear about my new job here. I think she knew your aunt who lived in this house."

She'd been my great-aunt, but I didn't correct him. "Sure, please text that to me. I might have a little time to drop by tomorrow, if that's okay."

Kylie started shutting off the lights over the coffee bar. "You can just leave your mug in the washer when you're done," she told August.

He frowned. "I hate to waste it, but I can't handle that much caffeine at night. I guess I should've made decaf." He headed over to dump it out in the sink.

Kylie hitched her small black backpack over a shoulder and walked toward the door. "See you all later."

"Thanks again for coming tonight," I said. "It went well." As well as could be expected, I supposed, with Milo on the warpath. Maybe Kylie's little pep talk would inspire him to keep his sharp tongue in check at work.

August placed the empty mug in the dishwasher and headed my way. "Thank you again, Miss Hatfield.

I'll let Gran know you might drop in tomorrow." His serious eyes met mine. "And please don't worry about things between Milo and me. I won't lie—I don't like him slamming my dad every chance he gets, but I realize it's coming from a place of insecurity. For the most part, we keep to ourselves in the cafe, and when we have to work alongside each other, I'll do all I can to keep tensions to a minimum."

"I'm impressed with your maturity." Unable to control my curiosity, I asked, "Is Bristol aware of Milo's behavior toward you? Are they still dating, do you know? I could ask her myself, but that might seem rude."

"They are, although he hasn't officially asked her to be his girlfriend." There was something in August's eyes that I couldn't quite read. "We don't really talk about her dating habits. Her brother and I just game together sometimes."

"I see." I led him toward the door. "You can go out this way. I'll lock up after you, then head into my place from inside. Thanks for training with Kylie tonight. You seem to be picking up the barista duties quickly, and you've done well with the shelter dogs, too."

"Thanks." He gave me a grateful smile, then ducked out the front door.

As I locked up and walked toward my section of the house, I considered August's personality. He really didn't seem the type to try to poison someone.

It was hard to guess if Robbie's murderer had cold-bloodedly planned to poison him with eye drops, or if they'd grabbed the bottle out of their bag and realized they could be used as a fatal weapon. Either way, I couldn't see how August would have dared to squirt a bunch of drops into a latte with everyone standing around.

As always, Coal was sitting on the other side of the connector door, anxiously awaiting my return. He always recognized when my steps were approaching, as opposed to anyone else's. Every now and then, when someone in the cafe walked a little too close to the door, a warning growl would erupt from the other side. And goodness help them if they happened to touch the doorknob.

He took his guard dog job seriously, which I appreciated, especially since I'd had a few run-ins with unsavory people during my recent years in Lewisburg.

As he stood and completely blocked my path, I gave him a pat on the head and eased around him. I led him toward the back door, so he could take a bathroom break while I did some online research into Rosie's Refuge. It never hurt to be prepared, and I could only hope that Rosetta might give me more insight into August and his father. I didn't want to blindly back our new employee in the police investigation, but at the same time, there had to be more elements at play in Robbie's poisoning than the Blackwells' disgust with their land-grabbing neighbor.

9

S ince Friday was my day off, I drove over to Rosie's Refuge around ten. It was well-hidden, tucked away in a deep woods off a winding side road. It would've been impossible to find if August hadn't given me explicit instructions, largely because the road didn't even have a sign labeling it. I understood the reason for the seclusion, though, since Rosetta probably took in women whose husbands or boyfriends were a threat to them and their children.

A deep rose hedge lined the front porch stretching around the older home. Plush peach, white, and magenta blooms nodded from strong stems. The pungent smell of fresh mulch drifted up to me, and I spotted a complex watering system tucked beneath the wood chips. August certainly took his gardening job seriously. I felt a compelling urge to pluck a drooping thick-petaled apricot bloom and tuck it behind my ear, but fought it off.

As I knocked on the blue front door, I wondered if the roses would get frosted before Bo and Summer's wedding in early October. If not, maybe Summer could ask about buying some for her bouquets or floral displays. They were definitely showstoppers, and the peach would fit in with her color scheme.

Voices approached from the other side of the door, and a large man opened it. I guessed that he had to be Owen Blackwell, because he looked like a taller, beefier version of August. Yet his narrowed green eyes differed from his son's brown ones.

"Yes?" he asked curtly.

Rosetta bustled up behind him and placed a hand on his shoulder. "This is Macy Hatfield," she explained. "Remember, August told us she'd be dropping by today?" She stepped forward, extending a slim hand. "Please, do come in, Miss Hatfield. We're glad to have you. I'll take you into the sitting room."

Her silver hair was cut into a stylish bob, which made her seem all the more elegant with her tailored silk blouse. Her eyes held some of the same shrewdness as her son's, but her smile was genuine.

Owen backed out of the way so we could walk past, but I could almost feel pent-up anger radiating from him. He shot me an unwilling half-smile, but I could tell he didn't really care to have me on the premises. Didn't he understand I'd come here to learn how to better defend his son? Given the way Owen was acting, I wouldn't blame the police for checking into his alibi on the day Robbie was poisoned. He came off like some kind of hothead.

As we walked toward the sitting room, I caught sight of a delicate-looking blonde woman standing by the staircase. She turned, exposing one of her smooth, tan cheeks that was puckered with angry white scar tissue. She gave a slight wave, and just as I was about to return it, I realized she'd directed it at Owen, not me.

Rosetta veered into the sitting room, and Owen edged around me to speak with the blonde. The tone he used with her was completely different—easy and calm—and there was a clear current of attraction between them. I recalled that he was an early widower, so some women might find his powerful, brooding persona fascinating. Hopefully he didn't lean *too* Heathcliff from *Wuthering Heights*, though.

Rosetta sat down in the same floral chair she'd used for the interview. It was situated in front of a bay window, so sunlight filtered through the sheer curtains and lit her hair like a halo. It seemed a fitting crown for someone who'd invested her own time and resources into helping women escape desperate situations.

I settled into a nearby loveseat and offered her a grateful smile. "Thank you for letting me drop in on such short notice. August has been doing a great job at the cafe. He told me he tends your roses, as well? They're beautiful."

Rosetta nodded. "My grandson works hard, no matter what he does. He's intense about everything he sets his hand to. I can't fathom how he manages to balance college classes, a job, and coming out here to work on my roses, but he seems to thrive on the action. I guess he likes to stay busy, like his father."

I decided to step into the opening she'd provided. "I heard Owen was widowed young," I said. "That must have been so hard on both of them."

She dropped her gaze to the floor, pressing a fist to her lips. "Valerie was so full of life—she never backed down from a challenge. She fought her cancer valiantly, and Owen was right there with her, every step of the way. When she passed, something inside him died, as well."

"I'm so sorry." Auntie A had died of cancer, but it hadn't been a prolonged process. That would be so heartbreaking to watch.

She blinked back tears, then looked up at me. "I've been praying that he will find his joy in life again, and I see flickers of it coming back."

I didn't want to cast aspersions on her son, but it seemed a fitting time to bring up his strained relationship with Robbie. "I heard his neighbor was giving him problems," I said.

Her lips hardened. "Robbie Sears. He's never been worth a dime. He was always trying to steal Owen's land—land he needs for his cattle." She templed her fingers together and her gaze turned fierce. "Let's just say that I hear things in my position, and I know for a fact that he beat his ex-wives. The man was a menace to society, and I can't say I'm particularly sorry he's dead."

Rosetta certainly wasn't making any bones about her animosity toward Robbie, but I could understand why. She'd seen enough battered women in her lifetime—and she'd been one herself—so I trusted her to recognize a wrong 'un when she saw one.

Her gaze softened. "I understand you're divorced. Was your ex...hateful to you?"

Rosetta's kind voice and empathetic nature brought unexpected tears to my own eyes. "He never harmed me," I assured her. "He was just the charmer type—you know, love 'em and leave 'em."

She nodded. "It still hurts," she said gently.

I needed to drastically shift conversational gears before she had me outright weeping. "August told you that Robbie was poisoned?" I asked, a bit too brusquely.

She leaned back in her chair. "He did. And he told me that Detective Hatcher wanted to ask him some questions, since he was the last to serve a drink to Robbie. Of course, Charlie is barking up the wrong tree. I can't believe he'd even consider my grandson a suspect." Her voice held an edge that said no one had better mess with August.

"He'll be looking into everyone, I can assure you. Charlie is thorough when it comes to crime."

She frowned. "They ought to be looking into that Eli Hooten. From the time he started dating Robbie's ex, Cora, he couldn't stand Robbie. Now those two are married, and thick as thieves in their hatred for him."

I thought back to how Cora shouted curses at

Robbie when he entered the joust ring. She certainly hadn't kept her feelings in check then. Rosetta might be looking in the right direction.

Owen tried to walk into the sitting room as a dark-haired boy dodged around his legs. The large man pretended to ignore the flitting child, who was practically braying with laughter. Obviously, there were more sides to Owen Blackwell than he cared to show. Auntie A always said that if kids and dogs liked a person, they were probably trustworthy.

"Lunch is served," Owen announced, wincing as the boy crashed into his knee. "Will you be staying for it, Miss Hatfield?"

The look he gave me was half-inquisitive, half-foreboding, as if he wanted to talk with me, but also didn't want me anywhere near the shelter. Again, he reminded me of Heathcliff.

I decided to put him out of his misery. "No, I can't stay, but thank you." I looked over at Rosetta and stood. "Thank you again for opening your doors for me. Please keep in touch—I'd like to do some kind of a fundraiser for Rosie's Refuge at the cafe. Maybe around Christmastime."

Rosetta smiled and stood. "You have a good heart, Macy. We would appreciate that, since we do purchase gifts for our women and children."

The boy briefly halted his shenanigans to shoot her a winning grin, and she stepped over to ruffle his thick hair. "They're precious gifts themselves."

Owen surprised me by leading the way to the front

door. As I stepped onto the porch, he muttered, "August likes his job."

I wasn't exactly sure how to respond to that. "I'm glad to hear that," I said finally.

He gripped the sides of the doorframe, making his body seem almost as wide as the door. "I figure you'll take care of him."

It sounded like a command, and I didn't care to be told what to do. Besides, I couldn't promise him anything. August would be under suspicion until Charlie ruled him out as a suspect.

I placed a hand on my hip. "Well, as long as he works with the police, I'm sure things will be fine." I hoped he could read the warning in my tone. His son had better be willing to answer questions, instead of fighting the system—which is what his father might advise.

His gaze dodged toward the rose bush on my left. "Yeah." He turned and headed into the house, firmly pulling the door closed behind him.

I had no idea what to make of the widower Owen Blackwell, but after our interaction today, I could see where Milo was coming from when he insinuated that he was a troublemaker. His attitude wouldn't do him any favors if Charlie came knocking on his farm door.

But for some inexplicable reason, I found myself hoping the homicide investigation wouldn't lead in that direction.

10

I grabbed lunch at the Chick-fil-A drive through, anxious to get home and decompress from my visit with a large cup of sweet tea.

Once I'd eaten and Coal started dozing off on the couch, I realized I had more questions that needed answers. My go-to for town information was my neighbor, so I headed next door to Vera's yellow two-story house.

As I'd guessed, she was sitting outside in her wicker chair, as she often did when the weather was pleasant. But as the rest of her porch came into view, I was irritated to see that Matilda Crump had also come for a visit. She was the first to call out to me as I walked in Vera's gate.

"Why, isn't this just the bee's knees, Vera? Macy is stopping in to see you."

Vera gave a nod as Waffles raced toward me, her entire body wagging in delight. "Sorry, dear," Vera said.

"I left her out while we were sitting. I hope she doesn't bother you too much."

I patted the golden curls on the friendly doodle's head. "I'm sure she won't."

Taking a seat closer to Vera, I turned to Matilda. "What brings you over today?"

Matilda lived the next street over, but she liked to take regular walks, even though she required a cane to go any distance. I should've guessed she would've dropped in around lunchtime, since Vera nearly always had something tasty prepared.

"We were discussing our upcoming book club read." Matilda made it sound like an exclusive experience, even though I'd spoken at their club this past Christmas and had been invited back numerous times since. "Since many of our members are taking vacations, they wanted something lighter." Her lip curled at the thought.

"We've decided on *The Pale Horse* by Agatha Christie." Vera was clearly excited about this choice, and no wonder. The club often chose heavier classics to plow through, and Vera had told me she was a slow reader. "Do you want to borrow my copy, Macy? You know we'd love to have you."

"It will be at my house this time," Matilda added. I wasn't sure if she was trying to discourage me or tempt me to attend. "Of course, we expect all our members to actually *read* the book. TV and movie adaptations are never up to par."

I reminded myself that Matilda was condescending

to everyone, not just to me. "Oh, of course. But I doubt I'll be able to make it that evening."

Vera gave me a curious look, as if realizing they hadn't even given me a date to attend.

Matilda's gaze sharpened. "Are you having a good time working at that faire? I do believe that Vera here will become a regular, what with Randall working over there." She cleared her throat. "It hardly seems an appropriate place for a woman of our maturity to frequent, though. A gaggle of grown adults playing dress-up and eating fire and the like."

The insults just kept on coming. I opened my mouth to respond, but Vera cut in.

"I like dressing up, Matilda. You'd be surprised at how many people our age are there. Why, Hattie Jessup is selling her apple butter and spicy venison jerky at one of those booths, and she told me she made two hundred dollars in one day!"

Matilda remained unimpressed. "Hattie's never had any compunctions about trying to turn a profit. Next thing you know, she'll be selling off her daughter's porcelain doll collection." She grabbed her cane and struggled to her feet before I could help her. Pointing the cane tip at me, she said, "Just let me know if you decide to attend the book club this time. I'll need to increase the head count for those bringing food."

As Matilda lumbered down the steps, Waffles maintained her sedate position by Vera's feet. Even though she was one of the ditziest dogs I'd ever come across, she still had the good sense to keep her distance from Matilda Crump.

Once Matilda had barged out of the gate, Vera said, "I'm sorry about that. She's always so rude, but you know she's on nearly every committee in town, so I can't avoid her."

I couldn't help but chuckle. "She sure is one of a kind."

"How about a nice glass of tea?" she offered. "I brewed a fresh pitcher in the fridge."

"I just had some, but thank you." I leaned back in my chair. "I wondered what you could tell me about Owen Blackwell or his mother. I think she knew Aunt Athaleen."

"Ah, yes. Rosetta. She's several years older than me, and she's been settled in these parts for years. She does a lot of good for the community with that shelter of hers. We make monthly donations to it through our Lamp Lighters Bible study—she's in the group." She watched a hummingbird as it darted from low pine branches to her porch feeder. "As for Owen, she worries about him. His wife's death just broke his heart."

"I met him today," I said. "Do you know anything about his problems with his neighbor, Robbie Sears?"

Vera rolled her eyes. "Oh, I know plenty about Robbie. Randall's had to keep a sharp eye on him at the fairgrounds. The way he carries on with those young mermaids is revolting. No woman should be subjected to that kind of behavior. Why, Randall had to intervene when Robbie jumped into the lagoon to chase one of them. He and his friends practically had to drag Robbie out of there. Disgraceful."

I cringed, thinking of the older knight splashing around with the twenty-something mermaids. "That's awful."

She nodded. "He's a menace—or should I say, he *was* a menace. Randall told me that he died in that joust. I can't say I felt too sorry for him."

It was starting to seem like no one did.

Shooting me a dark look, she added, "Randall also heard there was an incident up in the fairy forest on the day he died. He actually got himself banned from their area."

This was a very relevant piece of information, and one Charlie should be informed about. That would explain why Titan and I had seen the fairies gathered in a circle, looking distressed.

"Did he hear what happened?" I asked.

She nodded. "Apparently, Robbie manhandled a younger fairy named Amber when she wouldn't agree to meet him after hours. I know her—she's a sweet girl who used to be in my Sunday school class. Innocent and trusting, so of course, that predator Robbie made a beeline for her." Shaking her head, she added, "According to Randall, the fairies immediately kicked him out and circled around her. Some woman in a Phantom of the Opera mask offered to take her home, and his ex, Deanna, and another fairy said they'd talk to the fairground committee about getting him fired."

So Robbie had been on his way out. That was great, although he hardly seemed the type to care what anyone thought—he was just your everyday, classic abusive narcissist. He probably would've landed on his feet and talked his way into another job.

But, given the way he'd swanned around the fairgrounds being obnoxious to the young women, he had to have made enemies. And two of his ex-wives had been on the grounds on the day he died.

"What do you know about Robbie's ex-wives?" I asked, as Waffles inched closer to my leg. She pressed her body against my knee and angled her sad gaze my way, as if she might faint dead away if I didn't pet her. I gave in, rubbing behind her floppy ears.

"Well now, he's had three, hasn't he? At least the last time I counted. I can't understand how he manages to hook those poor women in the first place. He doesn't have a faithful bone in his body. I mean he *didn't*," she corrected.

"I know about Deanna and Cora," I said. "But who's the third wife?"

"That was a long time back—she doesn't live here now, so you wouldn't have met her. Her name is Iris Privett, and she grew up in these parts. I believe she married Robbie when she was quite young, but it didn't last long. Soon after they divorced, she moved out to the big city to be an accountant. Come to think of it, her mother died just a couple of weeks ago. She lived in that two-story brick house next to the church." She took a sip of tea, watching two hummingbirds fight for the feeder. "The thing about Iris is that she went into that marriage with the most beautiful features...then she came out of it with a scar across one cheek. You can do the math as to how that might've come about." She flattened her lips, as if she'd like to beat Robbie herself.

I had just seen someone with a scarred face, and she was lovely. "Do you know if Iris is in town now, by any chance?"

"Hm. I suppose she might be in so she can clean out her mother's things. Lawsie, but Ellie was a real packrat. Almost the opposite of her daughter in that way."

"Do you really believe Robbie might've cut her face?"

She stared into the distance. "Things got hushed up really fast when she wound up in the ER with that cut. Mind you, I wasn't living in the area at the time, but my nurse friend Liza happened to be working a hospital shift that afternoon. She said that Iris told some story about running into barbed wire wrapped around a tree in the woods. But Liza always swore that Iris' cut had to be made with a knife—and a serrated knife, at that."

My stomach twisted at the thought of someone inflicting that kind of damage intentionally. "That's sadistic. Did he harm his other wives, do you know?"

She shook her head. "Never heard tell of it, but Randall might be a better person to ask. He keeps track of men like that, since his late wife came out of an abusive marriage. Thank goodness she married him and got the opposite of her first husband. Randall is compassionate to a fault. Sometimes I think he'd do about anything I asked him to." She gave me an embarrassed smile and fell silent.

Waffles gave a sudden snort against my hand, trying to get my attention. I gave her a final pat and stood. "Thank you, Vera. That's been really helpful. I'll try to talk with Randall tomorrow at the faire."

"He'll be glad to have you stop by," she said. She eased to her feet. "I'd better head inside and get myself a little snack so I can get cracking on *The Pale Horse*. If I don't read every page, Matilda will sniff it out."

I laughed as I headed toward her gate, Waffles on my heels. "I can believe it."

11

Titan and I spent Friday evening together, first eating at a new restaurant in White Sulphur Springs, then bringing our boxed tiramisu home so we could watch the 1996 *Twister* movie. Somehow, Titan had missed seeing it back in the day, so he had no idea of how one Dodge Ram would change the tornado-tracking world. I'd coveted a Ram after seeing that movie, but could never justify the expense.

Once we'd finished our movie and dessert, I suggested brewing up some decaf house blend coffee. Titan agreed, walking over to "help," which actually consisted of standing next to the counter and appreciatively watching me putter around. He did manage to set out a couple of mugs, though.

Coal trotted over to his dog bed and started kneading it before he cozied up. He was clearly ready to call it a night, but he wasn't about to neglect his guard duty and head upstairs, no matter how much he liked Titan. He had to keep me in his sights—which was ironically just like Titan himself.

Trying to hide my grin, I headed over to grab the creamer. My phone rang, and I saw that Bo was on the other end.

"Hey, sis. I hate to bother you so late, but we'll need to get someone to fill in for August tomorrow at the faire. I wasn't sure who would be available." He sighed. "Charlie wants him to head down to the station for questioning."

"No," I protested. "Why?"

"I guess someone reported that August said in public that it's not surprising when land disputes turn violent, and that he hoped Robbie got what was coming to him for stealing his dad's land."

"*Someone* reported it?" I groaned. "I'll bet I know exactly who that someone is."

Titan's eyes widened at my scathing tone, but he stayed silent, taking the creamer and pouring the right amount into each coffee mug.

Bo continued. "I don't know who it was, since Charlie didn't say. But I do think he's concerned about August. Young men can be a little impulsive, you know."

He didn't have to tell me. Bo had joined the Marines as soon as he could, ready for adventures that would take him out of his mountain home. He'd discovered his strengths as a Marine, then he'd moved on to work for the Drug Enforcement Administration, finally landing his ten-year cover job at Coffee Mass on the West Coast.

But August seemed more certain about direction in life, which was heading toward forensic investigation. And he was firmly attached to his family farm and to his grandmother's shelter. I couldn't see him chucking any one of those things to poison his neighbor.

Still, Charlie had to do what he had to do. "I'll get in touch with Bristol," I said. "I think she's free tomorrow. She's worked our booth before, so I won't need to tell her much, but I'll help her out until Kylie comes for her shift after lunch."

"I'll be there as well, so we shouldn't get too inundated," he said.

"You planning to wear the kilt?" I asked.

I could practically hear his eyes roll. "Yes, but I refuse to squeeze my legs into those wool knee socks again, and I'm wearing a tee. I don't know how those Scotsmen did it—I thought they had a similar climate to ours."

"They must've been made of tougher stuff than you, bro," I joked.

Titan wrinkled his brow, probably wondering if Bo would let this comment pass. But of course, he did.

"Very funny. I'll see you in the morning, my Viking sister."

"I might shake things up a little tomorrow," I said. "You might not even recognize me. Have a good night. I love ya."

Titan shot me a curious look as I set the phone on

the counter. "You're wearing something different tomorrow?"

"Yes—I've been inspired by Vera, believe it or not. I remembered that I have a bridesmaid dress I only used once, but it was actually quite pretty. Kind of a pistachio green color that looks Roman. I could wear my leather sandals and some of my gold coin jewelry and maybe pull off a Roman noblewoman look."

"You could put your hair up." He couldn't hide his admiring gaze. "You have such a lovely neck."

I blushed. "Thank you."

He put down his coffee mug and stepped in so close, I could hear his soft, steady breathing. He gently brushed a wayward wave off my cheek and tucked it behind my ear. "I hate that I have to go back to Virginia on Sunday." He leaned down and slowly kissed my cheek, which was somehow more stirring than a kiss on the lips.

My cheeks flushed again, so I buried my hot face in his chest. "I'll miss you," I said, my voice charged. Each visit was making it harder for me to tell him goodbye, and each visit we were getting closer to a commitment I wasn't certain I was ready for.

But Titan's tight embrace temporarily choked out my doubts, so I stood there for some time, savoring the cedar scent of his cologne and letting his unwavering loyalty fill my emotional love tank once again.

BRISTOL ARRIVED at the faire bright and early, wearing an outfit inspired from her favorite anime movie, *Kiki's Delivery Service*. She wore a blue dress with a large red bow in her dark hair, and she carried a broom and a stuffed black cat. I hadn't watched the movie, but it was easy to see that she'd nailed the look of the main character, since many of the fairgoers stopped to squeal over her.

I figured Milo had told Bristol very little about his rivalry with August. Last night, I hadn't specified why August had to miss work today, but I felt that Bristol had the right to know what was going on. I started filling her in as I wiped out the coffee bean hopper.

She swept her glossy hair over her shoulder so forcefully, she nearly dislodged her red bow. "You have *got* to be kidding me," she said. "Why is Milo acting so mean toward August?"

I supposed I'd have to spell it out for her. "I think he feels envious of your friendship."

She turned to take a woman's order, then lowered her voice as she faced me again. "But that's all it is— friendship." She pulled one of Charity's chocolate croissants out of the bakery display and started wrapping it.

Once she'd rung up the customer, I explained that August had to go into the police station for questions today, and I shared what someone had "helpfully" reported that he'd said. "Did he ever mention his neighbor to you?" I asked.

She leaned against the counter. "I mean, he did

occasionally, but it was just because it bothered him to see his dad getting treated that way. They were going to sue him over taking their land, I think. But that was the extent of it. His dad can definitely take care of his own issues."

Bo shifted behind the counter, and I realized he'd been waylaid by a woman who was asking him flirty questions about his clan. She looked like she was about to squeeze his bicep when I stepped toward her and intervened.

"I'll be happy to ring you up now, ma'am," I interjected. "And I'd love to give you one of these flyers from our local shelter." I handed her one, allowing Bo to shift out of her reach.

Once she'd trudged over to my side of the counter, Bo prepped her iced coffee and handed it over. When she was finally out of sight—for now—Bo gave me a relieved smile, and I turned back to Bristol.

"He'd never be impolite to a customer," I whispered. "But she was definitely taking some liberties."

Bristol grinned, still looking a little distracted. "You have to admit, y'all did get some nice genetics."

Bo's phone dinged with a text, so he glanced at it. "It's August," he mouthed. After reading it, he seemed to think for a moment, then texted back. Once he got off the phone, he walked me over to a tree to talk. Bristol politely busied herself with straightening the bottled drink cooler.

"August said he's heading home—the police aren't keeping him. But he feels like someone is trying to set him up. His dad is concerned that his going in for questioning might somehow jeopardize the position he's landed at the State Police Forensic Lab next summer, especially if people keep feeding the police lies about him."

"So he didn't say those things about land disputes turning violent and Robbie getting what was coming to him?" I asked.

"Not exactly, but he didn't word things in such a pointed way. He told Charlie that he would never poison someone, especially over a dispute that's already in court. His dad wondered if I could recommend a good lawyer in case August gets pulled in again. Understandably, he doesn't want his son's career dreams to get torpedoed due to police suspicion."

"You put him in touch with Gilbert?" Gilbert Davis defied every heartless lawyer joke out there, because he was as honest as the day was long. Although he was gentle with his clients, he was also a force to be reckoned with and had a backbone of steel in the courtroom.

"I sure did. His dad was grateful." Bo looked thoughtful. "Owen's been a firestarter during some town meetings, but I feel like he always has Lewisburg's best interests at heart. I actually enjoy it when he shows up, because I know I'll learn something, and he's never been antagonistic toward me as mayor."

"I'm guessing he could be pretty intimidating though, if he wanted to be," I observed.

Bo grinned. "He is a big guy, but I could take him, sis."

Of course Bo would boil it all down to brute strength. I had no doubt my brother could outmaneuver Owen in a hand-to-hand combat situation, but I wondered if Owen's blustery persona might have gotten out of hand in regard to Robbie Sears. At the very least, I was hoping that Charlie had also checked into Owen's whereabouts on the day Robbie was poisoned.

12

Since Titan was having lunch with Julius, I decided to use my break to do a little fairground sleuthing on behalf of August. I was becoming more and more convinced our newest employee had neither the wherewithal nor the motivation to risk his forensic degree and poison Robbie.

Cosmic Crystal—aka Deanna—was my first stop. She was sitting outside her tent, just as she had the day she'd spoken with Robbie. She set down her container of onion rings and motioned me over, her bracelets jangling. She wasn't wearing her turban today, and her thin, tomato-red hair straggled around her shoulders.

"Come in, my dear girl," she urged. "I'd be happy to give you a free palm-reading, since you're a fellow tradesman at the faire."

I had no intention of getting my palm read or any other such malarkey. "Actually, I just dropped in to talk to you about Robbie. You said you'd read his cards and told him he was in danger on the day he collapsed? I've been hearing some rumors about the way he was carrying on with women at the faire. Was he by any chance harassing you or anything?"

Her gaze sharpened under her sparkly purple eyelids. "We were having a disagreement, sure, but he wasn't harassing me. I'd invited him in to get his cards read, and that's when I flipped the Death card. I tried to convince him it wasn't a joke, and that he needed to be careful, but as usual, he just wrote off what I had to say. After that, I followed him outside, where you saw us arguing."

It threw a slightly different angle on things that Deanna had invited Robbie into her tent, instead of reading the cards beforehand and accosting him outside. Was it possible she was still carrying a torch for her ex, and that she'd wanted to spend time with him that day?

Trying to better understand her motivations, I said, "You were quick to come to his aid on the jousting field. It seems like you cared a lot for him."

She gave a regretful nod. "I wanted to watch his joust, because I had a terrible feeling something would go wrong." Wiping her fingers on her napkin, she added, "I had no idea he would die out there."

Technically, he didn't die until his organs shut down later in the hospital, but I didn't want to point that out. I tried a different tack.

"I heard that he harassed a young fairy the day he died—Amber, I believe? Did you know about that?" It was a trick question, because Vera had already reported that Deanna had been up at the fairy forest to comfort Amber afterward.

Deanna's eyes dropped. "Unfortunately, yes. She's such a sweet girl. I was visiting with my friend up in the forest when Robbie grabbed Amber. The poor girl managed to slip from his grip, but she was so upset, she couldn't stop shaking. We all tried to help her, and I told her we'd make sure it didn't happen again. But she was still nervous about working up there." She thoughtfully munched on an onion ring, then looked up at me. "She was the one you saw at my tent after Robbie's accident. She was shaken by it, so I offered her a cup of my calming lavender tea."

"I'm sure that helped." She'd answered my question honestly, which I appreciated.

She straightened in her chair, frowning. "Well, Robbie really overstepped. I don't know what got into him this year, but he kept making a nuisance of himself on the fairgrounds."

I found it hard to believe this was the first time he'd harassed women at the fair. Men like that had patterns of behavior that only intensified over time. His other wife would have been aware of this, as well.

"Did Cora also see him attack Amber?" I asked.

Deanna shook her head. "No, she was getting Eli ready for the joust. She's utterly devoted to her new husband, and she won't give Robbie the time of day. I don't think she ever cared for him in the first place. She's a moneygrubber, and she got a little surprise when she found out she wasn't getting her hands on Robbie's horse breeding business in the divorce settlement." She gave a haughty smile. "I'm the one listed as co-owner, since Robbie and I built that business together."

I took that as my cue to leave. It was hard to read Deanna—on the one hand, she still seemed to care for Robbie, but on the other, she'd recognized that he'd gone too far in harassing Amber.

"Thanks for your time. I appreciate it." I turned toward the main path.

"Drop by anytime. I'll be happy to tell your fortune, free of charge," she said.

That was never going to happen, but I gave her a friendly nod goodbye.

I hesitated, then decided to head over to Randall's leatherworking booth. He seemed to be the eyes and ears of this place, and he probably hadn't missed a thing on the day Robbie was poisoned. He might have some information Charlie had missed.

RANDALL's thick gray curls looked even more unruly than usual as I approached his booth. He wore a tan leather vest and brown chaps that made him look like a kindly cowboy.

"Good to see you, Macy," he said. "Vera said you paid her a visit yesterday. She was glad to have a break from Matilda." He grinned.

I shot him an understanding smile, stepping onto the platform where he'd set up his wares. "It's always refreshing to hang out with Vera." Fingering a leather knife sheath, I said, "I have a few questions for you, if you have a few minutes."

He glanced around. "It's pretty dead around lunchtime. Fire away." He peeled off one of his leather gloves, revealing a tattoo I'd never seen before.

It was a tattoo of a lion.

I was at a loss for words. Surely Randall wasn't the tattooed knight who'd run from me in the woods? He seemed a bit taller, and to my knowledge, he didn't have a handy knight suit tucked away anywhere. I scrambled to come up with a question, but my mind had suddenly gone blank.

He followed my gaze to his hand. "It's a new tattoo," he offered. "Vera wasn't crazy about it, but I told her I must be having a late-life crisis. I was too busy to have a midlife one."

"It's nice," I said. "I've always found lions fascinating."

"They look out for each other," he said simply.

For the first time, I realized that there was something quietly protective about Randall. The way he'd been observing Robbie's bad behavior on the fairground evidenced his investment in the safety of others.

I waded in with my questions. "Vera said you saw Robbie flirting with lots of women. I guess you heard about what he did in the fairy forest pretty soon after it happened?"

He nodded. "A bunch of vendors were talking about it. Like me, a lot of them felt like it was the last straw. Vera told you about the mermaid lagoon incident, didn't she? That was clownish enough. Then Robbie had the absolute gall to go and put his hands on that fairy, Amber. Why, she's young enough to be his granddaughter." He stepped in close and lowered his voice. "Once I heard about that, I called up my friend Jed—he owns the faire, and his wife Angie is in charge of the hiring and firing. I told him they'd better do something about Robbie that very day, or they'd start getting slapped with harassment lawsuits. Rob assured me he would be banned from the grounds. So it was Robbie's last joust, in more ways than one." He gave me a satisfied look.

"I'm glad you did something about it," I said.

"He thought he was so slick he could get away with it," Randall continued. "But I've heard that he was physically abusive in all his marriages. Men like that are a scourge on society."

I nodded. "Thanks for filling me in, Randall—and thanks for looking out for womankind. Will Vera be dropping in today?"

He shook his head. "She decided not to get all dressed up again. I think Matilda put a damper on her enthusiasm." He brightened. "But I'll be taking her out to her favorite steakhouse tonight."

It was adorable to see how he doted on my neighbor, who was like a grandmother to me. "She'll love that. Let me guess—she'll be ordering chicken tenders and honey mustard."

He chuckled. "You know her well. She's not one for steak at a steakhouse, but I sure am. I'll have a medium rare ribeye coming my way."

"You all have a great time." I checked my phone as I walked away, realizing that my lunch break was quickly dwindling. I needed to head back to our booth and grab one of Charity's sandwiches, since I hadn't taken the time to pack something.

But on my way around the lagoon, I caught sight of Cora. She was sitting in the royal booth near the jousting ring, and she seemed to be observing me. When I looked at her directly, she whipped her head the other way.

Not wanting to miss my chance, I headed straight toward her, trying to come up with some pretense to engage her in conversation. As the platform came into view, I decided that Cora was probably the type who appreciated someone who was up-front, so I shielded my eyes from the sun and introduced myself to her.

"Hi, I'm Macy Hatfield—I saw you over at our Barks & Beans Cafe booth the other day. You were talking with Robbie Sears," I said.

She didn't look embarrassed in the least, even though she'd been reaming him out that day. "Yes, I remember," she said. "I keep meaning to visit your cafe in town. I'd like to get a new dog someday, and Eli thinks we should get a shelter dog. I used to have the sweetest Boxer, but he died last year."

I described some of the shelter dogs we'd had lately, then gently steered back to the topic of her ex. "I couldn't help but notice there was some animosity between you and Robbie that day," I said.

She laughed. "I know I shouldn't speak ill of the dead, but he deserved everything he got. He was a fool and a petty tyrant."

I heard the sound of quiet footsteps approaching, so I turned to see who it was.

Eli stepped forward to shake my hand. "You run that dog cafe, don't you? I met your brother the other day. He seems like a nice guy, and I've heard he's a really competent mayor."

I hated to admit it, but his compliments of my brother were disarming, making me feel favorable toward him. As he stepped forward to rub the knots out of Cora's neck, I was even more inclined to think that Eli was a decent guy. Cora seemed to have chosen wiser the second time around.

The king and queen were staring at me and shifting on their makeshift thrones, so I hurried along to my next question for Eli.

"You did a good job on that joust," I said. "Did you notice anything wrong with Robbie as he was riding?"

Eli's eyes darkened. "He wasn't up to par that day, but from what I heard, he'd been bothering some fairies just before that."

Cora broke in. "He got himself banned from the

fairy forest, and good on them for doing that. He needed a hefty dose of reality. You can't act like that on your job—even if it's only part-time. In fact, he shouldn't have acted like that anywhere."

The queen shot me a regally irritated look and stood to stretch. I supposed I was blocking her view of the empty jousting ring.

"Okay, well, it was nice to meet you all," I said. "Be sure to drop by the cafe sometime—I'm sure you'll find a doggie companion you'll love."

Eli smiled, then turned an admiring gaze toward Cora. They seemed like two happy peas in a pod, but Robbie's loose cannon behavior must have driven them both to distraction. Could they have conspired together to rid the world of Cora's abusive ex?

13

As I headed back toward our booth, I considered what I'd learned, which wasn't much. No one seemed to like Robbie, with the possible exception of Deanna. But even she had admitted that he'd behaved abominably on the fairgrounds. While it seemed a little extreme to poison a predator like Robbie, far more had been done for far less.

When I arrived at our booth, Titan clanked as he stood from the bench. Once again, he'd worn his full armor.

"I'm trying to get my money's worth with this costume," he explained, awkwardly wrapping one metal-coated arm around me. "Today looked to be a little cooler, so I thought I could swing it."

I smiled up at his warm eyes. "You look great."

He glanced at my hair, which I'd twisted up into a loose knot, and then down at my Roman garb. "You look amazing. Maybe I should've come as a gladiator, so we could've matched."

The visual of my hulking boyfriend in a gladiator costume was a bit too much for me to process. I cleared my throat. "Maybe next year. You ready to get some lunch? I was thinking of grabbing one of Charity's Italian muffuletta sandwiches and a Knight Brew—in your honor, of course. I know you already had lunch with Julius, but I can grab a Knight Brew for you, if you want. It'll be on the house."

Titan gave a grateful nod as Bo walked our way.

"That'll be coming out of your paycheck, sis," he joked. "What were you doing on lunch break, if not eating?"

"Just talking to people like Randall," I said vaguely. I was smart enough to know that Bo would object to my prowling around the fairground so I could track down suspects in Robbie's death.

Bo and Titan shot me dubious looks, but I started humming and headed behind the counter to get my sandwich. My brother and Titan started up their own conversation.

Bristol's red bow had slid to one side, so I stepped over and adjusted it for her.

"Thanks," she said, her voice strained.

I took a closer look. She was staring blankly into the distance, her brown eyes wide.

I wrapped an arm around her and whispered, "Are you okay, sweetie?"

She gave a slow nod. "I just talked with my brother

Ethan—he's tight with August, you know. I needed to know if Milo was right in thinking that August liked me."

Before she even said it, I realized what the answer was and filled in the blanks. "He does."

With a wondering look, she said, "Apparently, he's had a thing for me since we were young, but he's never showed it or even said one word. I had no idea."

I could believe it. Milo, in some primal way, had sniffed out August's long-burning obsession with Bristol and decided he wasn't going to allow it.

"I need some time to think," Bristol murmured. "Do you care if I head on home? My shift's almost up. I'm not sure where Kylie is, though."

"Go ahead. I'm sure she'll get here soon."

As if on cue, Kylie strode through the gate and gave us a wave. She was dressed like a pirate, complete with an eye patch and a feathered tricorn hat. Predictably, she wore black leather breeches and a flowing black jacket. Her voluminous white blouse was her one non-black exception.

The cutlass tucked into her sheath looked remarkably real. Since she sold swords on the side, I had to wonder if she might've snuck a real one through the gates. But I decided that some things were better left unasked.

Kylie walked over and clapped Bristol on the shoulder. "Ahoy, matey."

Bristol broke into a relieved grin. "Ahoy. Have ye come to take over for me, land lubber?"

"That I have." Kylie cocked her hat to the side, so she could get a better look at Bristol with her one eye. Dropping her pirate accent, she asked, "Hey, did something happen? You look a little off."

Bristol nodded. "There's some stuff going on between Milo and August," she said. "But you probably already knew that."

Kylie pursed her lips. "Those two. They need to wise up."

"It's okay." Bristol turned to me. "I'll see you on Monday."

I patted her back. "Try not to worry about it. These things have a way of sorting themselves out." After I spoke the words, I stopped short, realizing Auntie A would've told me the exact same thing, had I found myself in Bristol's situation.

As Bristol walked away, Kylie gave a low whistle. "Like sands through the hourglass...so are the days of our lives."

I laughed. "You watch soap operas? I didn't even know you still could."

She shrugged. "I catch some reruns." With no further explanation, she started wiping down the countertop.

I grabbed my sandwich, then asked Kylie if she'd mind making a couple of Knight Brews. She nodded, then whipped them up in no time flat.

Once I had our food in hand, I walked Titan over to a table, so we could spend my final minutes of break together. I wasn't sure if he planned to wander around the fairgrounds until I joined him or stick close, but either way, it was nice to know he was around.

He took a drink and asked, "Was Bristol okay? She seemed worried about something."

"It'll be okay. Just a little cafe drama, that's all."

He gave a silent nod and prepared to take another bite, but out of nowhere, Cora came hurrying up to our table and fixed him with a stare.

Unnerved by her tense look, I asked, "What's going on?"

"We just figured out my trick show was scheduled directly after the joust. I was planning to stand in for Robbie and joust with Eli, but that won't leave me enough time to change and prep for my own show. We've been looking for knights, and believe it or not, you're the only one walking around in armor today." She gave him an appreciative once-over. "Plus, you really look the part. Would you be able to fill in for Robbie for just one joust? I'll be able to do it tomorrow."

Titan looked unusually dubious. "I'm not really a horseman," he said slowly.

Cora shot me a desperate look, as if willing me to convince him. "All you have to do is shout a few insults at Eli, mount a horse—she's super gentle—then ride toward him with your lance outstretched. The horse knows exactly what to do. You'll just tap Eli's shield every time you go by him, and he'll give you the win. It's all planned out."

Sensing Titan's hesitancy, I said, "Eli seemed to hit Robbie's shield pretty hard."

She shook her head. "That was how they'd practiced it. Eli wouldn't even touch...uh, what's your name, sir?"

"Titan McCoy," he answered.

"Titan," she breathed. "What a name." She cocked her head to the side and gave him a hopeful smile. "What do you say, Sir Titan?"

My boyfriend could sense a damsel in distress when he saw one. And he was too much of a gentleman to walk away when people were in need.

"Sure." He eased up into a standing position. "Tell me what I'll need to do to get ready."

Bo agreed that I should take a break to help Titan get set up for the show, which started in twenty minutes. We followed Cora over to the black horse that Robbie had ridden, which was named Pandora. Her name was hardly comforting.

After Titan made three failed attempts to hook his boot into the stirrup, I grew even more concerned. I helped him angle his unwieldy armor-clad body onto the saddle, but then he started sliding off the other side. Before I could scurry around to him, he'd taken a hard fall onto the ground, with one foot still stuck in the stirrup.

He allowed himself a mild groan, rubbing at his lower back. I hurried to ease his boot from the stirrup.

Cora shot me a desperate look. "I have to help Eli get ready. Are you able to handle this?"

She was basically asking if I work a quick miracle to get my boyfriend in riding condition, and I seriously doubted that could happen. But I gave her a nod and said, "I'll get him on there."

As she walked away, I helped Titan to his feet. He seemed to have trouble standing up straight. "I think I pulled something," he said.

I walked him closer to Pandora's side, where he again struggled to pull himself up. "Have you ever ridden before?" I asked, trying to push him upward.

"Once." His voice was tight as he shifted onto the saddle. "It was my neighbor's old horse, and it didn't like me. It tried to scrape me off on a tree limb, and it would've succeeded if my friend hadn't pulled it the other direction. I haven't been fond of horses since."

So he had zero real experience on horseback. The FBI probably hadn't trained him for it, either. I suspected his understated "I haven't been fond of horses" could have better been translated as, "I have a paralyzing fear of horses," but he would never in his life admit that.

"You know, you don't have to ride today." I gave Pandora a smoothing pat on her neck as Titan wormed his boots into the stirrups. "They can cancel the joust. People will understand."

He gave me a strained smile. "Well, I'm already up

here, and Pandora seems to be okay with me. I'll give it my best shot."

I gazed up at him. Sunlight lit the gold in his determined eyes as I passed his helmet up. He gave me a brief grin before pulling it down over his face. Thankfully, Pandora stood still, despite Titan's jerky movements.

I thought back to the short knight who'd helped Robbie onto his horse. He'd taken Robbie's water bottle, so it stood to reason that he'd been the one to hand it to him, as well.

Why wasn't that knight here today to serve in the same role for Titan?

It was becoming obvious that the knight must've been the one to poison Robbie, and most likely with the green water bottle. Robbie had been hale and hearty enough to harass Amber just before the joust, which hardly seemed likely if he'd been poisoned earlier. Then again, I had no idea how quickly those eye drops worked. Maybe I could finagle some details out of Charlie.

The trumpet blew, dragging me back into the stressful moment. Titan would be doing well not to fall off the horse in the first few minutes of the joust, but I plastered a cheery smile on my face that said otherwise.

When the announcer said it was five minutes until the death-defying joust between Sir Eli and Sir Titan, Pandora took a step forward. "Death-defying" wasn't the most heartening description of the upcoming event, but I supposed it upped the stakes for the viewers.

I could only hope the stakes stayed low for the riders. In particular, for my inexperienced boyfriend.

I glanced over to our cafe booth. Bo and Kylie had stepped out in order to see the joust. Bo probably knew that Titan was wet behind the ears when it came to equestrian ventures, since he was more familiar with Titan's range of experience than I was. He wanted to be on the scene, should his friend suddenly find himself unhorsed.

My stomach clenched as the second trumpet gave its short blast, and both riders trotted into the ring. I climbed over the fence rails to watch.

Eli shouted the first taunt. "It's time to have it out, you pigeon-livered peasant!"

We hadn't gone over anything clever for Titan to say, but he surprised me by firing back, "Idle prattle! Your brain is as dry as a biscuit!"

The crowd laughed. Eli rose in his seat, spurring his horse in our direction.

Titan lightly kicked into Pandora's flanks, and she, too, launched forward. He had managed to extend his lance, but now struggled to raise his shield. For a moment, he looked dreadfully off-balance, as if he were heading for a fall.

But he managed to right himself by leaning in closer to Pandora's neck, using her strong muscles to support the lance. By the time Eli clopped up close,

Titan was ready, and he struck his opponent's shield with a flourish.

The crowd went wild, and I clapped furiously.

The next two passes went off without a hitch. Titan seemed to get more and more invested in his showmanship with each pass. By the time he won, most of the crowd was cheering for him.

After the king crowned him the victor, Titan swung —or rather, creaked—off Pandora's saddle and walked to where I was standing. After removing his helmet, he stiffly knelt before me and offered up his floral winner's crown. The crowd broke into a frenzy, hooting and hollering.

Cheeks aflame, I accepted his wilting gift and pressed a kiss to his head. I was proud of my boyfriend, who had not only mastered horse riding in one day, but had also put on an entertaining show for the bystanders. I placed the oversized crown on top of my head and took Pandora's reins. Together, we led her toward the stable.

Once the crowd started to disperse, Eli and Cora walked our way. Cora was grinning, and Eli said, "You're welcome to fill in tomorrow, too. People loved you."

Cora bobbed her head. "Yeah—they never had that kind of response for Robbie, I can tell you."

At least neither of them seemed irritated that Titan had basically stolen the show.

Titan shook his head. "I'm afraid I'll be heading

home tomorrow. But thanks for an experience I won't soon forget."

Cora and Eli thanked Titan again and headed to the other side of the ring. In the meantime, a crowd of younger women raced our way, giggling and circling around Titan. My knight in shining armor appeared to have stolen a few hearts along with the show.

I hitched my arm under his metal gear and gave them an understanding—but dismissive—smile. "This valiant knight has earned some refreshment, wouldn't you agree, maidens?"

They giggled again, but cleared a path for Titan to awkwardly make his way to the Barks & Beans booth. In a reversal of roles, he clung to my arm as if he were about to keel over.

He gave a low groan. "I'm pretty sure I pulled muscles I didn't even know I had."

Deciding he needed something more comfortable —and unrecognizable—to wear, I helped him take a seat on our bench, then I headed toward Randall's booth. Surely my neighbor's boyfriend could loan us something for Titan to wear for the duration of the day. He'd given all he had to save the jousting show, and, although he'd never ask for sympathy, he deserved a break from knighthood.

14

R andall was more than happy to loan me an extra-long pair of leather pants and a loose, cotton peasant shirt for Titan. After Bo helped him shed his outer layer of armor, Titan headed into the port-a-potty so he could finish getting changed. When he returned to our booth, I had to catch my breath.

Titan looked like a pirate himself in his open-neck shirt, which he'd tucked into pants that fit him like a glove.

Bo chuckled and said, "You like what you see, sis?"

I realized I'd been standing there with my mouth open. "Very funny," I retorted, salvaging some of my dignity by shooting him a condescending look. "I'm just glad the clothes fit, that's all."

Titan stepped closer and cupped my neck with his hand. "Is that really all, my Roman queen?" he whispered into my ear.

If he kept this up, I'd be rendered powerless to keep

up with my basic tasks. "Maybe you should get something cold to drink, then walk off some of your aches and pains," I said.

He gave me a slow nod, as if realizing I needed to keep some distance from his captivating presence. "Sure. I keep meaning to watch that glassblower at work. He explains every step of the process."

Kylie offered him an iced latte and a shortbread cookie, which he gratefully accepted before walking away with some difficulty. She pulled up her pirate eye patch to shoot me a knowing look.

"You're head over heels for him, aren't you?" Without giving me time to answer, she added, "Joel looks at me that way, and it's totally disconcerting. Sometimes, I can't believe someone would like me so...completely."

Before we could talk more, Owen Blackwell walked over to Bo and shook his hand. "Thank you for recommending Gilbert Davis. He's talked with us and offered solid suggestions as to how we should proceed if August gets called in for more questioning." With his back to me, he rubbed a large hand across his collar, drawing attention to a neck tattoo I hadn't noticed when I visited the shelter.

It was a small-sized tattoo of a thickly maned lion.

I started mentally running down the list of people I'd seen with lion tattoos. First, the short knight with the hand tattoo, then Randall with his hand tattoo, and now Owen with a neck tattoo. Could all three be a coincidence?

I managed to hide my curious gaze before he turned to look at the food display. "I'm starving. Let's see—could I have one of those ham and brie sandwiches?"

Kylie nodded and bagged his food, then I rang him up. He gave me a slight nod of recognition, but didn't say anything.

As he took his food and walked toward the main path, I spoke quietly to Kylie. "What's with all the lion tattoos? I keep seeing them around."

It shouldn't have come as a surprise that Kylie knew exactly what I was talking about. "I've heard there's some kind of club in town that uses those tats to identify members. But no one will tell me what kind of a club it is. I'm determined to get to the bottom of it, though." She glanced toward Owen's retreating back. "And now I know August's dad has one, too. Interesting."

It certainly was.

TITAN RETURNED, requesting a water bottle before he eased onto the bench. "I'm not sure if I worked the kinks out or made things worse."

"I might have one of those instant heat packs in my purse," Kylie offered. "Let me check."

"And I have some ibuprofin," I said, digging into my bag. "You should take a couple—or maybe three, given your height."

He groaned, but allowed us to ply him with our remedies. After placing the heat pack against his lower back, he leaned back and sighed. "This didn't quite turn out the way I'd planned."

Before I could respond, someone in a Phantom of the Opera mask and a long black cloak swirled toward our counter. Vera had said that the Phantom had comforted Amber after Robbie's harassment, and I hadn't seen any other Phantoms walking the fairgrounds, so I greeted this one warmly. "Welcome to the Barks & Beans Cafe," I said. "I love your costume. That book was so mesmerizing to me as a teen."

The person, who was wearing long white gloves, gave a brief nod, then gestured toward the menu. "I'd like a medium Peasant's Honey iced coffee, please," she said.

Her voice was muffled by her white mask, but I felt like I recognized it from somewhere. "Coming right up," Kylie said.

Out of nowhere, Deanna hurried toward our counter and grabbed the Phantom's arm. "I need to talk with you," she said quietly. "Do you have a minute?"

The Phantom stared at her, but I couldn't determine if her look was friendly or foreboding. "I'm waiting for my coffee," she said.

Deanna gave a curt nod. "Just drop by on your way past," she commanded, then walked off.

The Phantom paid for her Peasant's Honey with cash, then walked directly toward Deanna's tent.

Kylie shot me a bewildered look. "Who was that?

She didn't seem too friendly. How does that fortune-teller know her?"

"I don't know." I peered toward the Cosmic Crystal tent. From my vantage point, I could see the Phantom walk under the awning and start speaking with Deanna. As she stood there, holding her Barks & Beans Cafe cup, I was struck with a sudden sense of déjà vu. Deanna gestured with her hands, much as she had with Robbie, and I wondered if she was about to foist another deadly fortune on the Phantom.

I was considering walking that way when Jimmy arrived, distracting me. He wore an old-style coal miner's hat and faded coveralls. He didn't look at all Medieval, but I was pleased he'd even bothered to dress up.

"Miss Macy," he said, giving me a polite nod.

I smiled. "Nice outfit."

"My wife picked it out for me. This was my daddy's hat—he was a miner over in Wyoming County." His look turned sober. "He watched one of his friends die in that mountain bump collapse over at Glen Rogers, back in the Fifties."

Catching what Jimmy said, Bo stepped over and gave him a respectful nod. "I'm sorry to hear that."

Kylie asked, "I've never heard of a mountain bump. What is that?"

Jimmy's eyes darkened. "It's a roof collapse. The pressure from above got to be too much, and the mine roof broke through its supports. It buried them in rubble. Five men in all—I think every day of how that could've been my daddy."

We all fell silent, unable to put into words how deeply these accidents affected us. Coal mining was woven into our West Virginia heritage, but it was also a constant reminder that the mountains that protected us also had the potential to kill.

Titan, who must have overheard the entire story, struggled to his feet and walked over. He clasped Jimmy on the arm and his voice broke a little. "I'm glad you could honor your father today."

As he tried to straighten up, I realized he seemed to be leaning on Jimmy for support.

"We'd better get you home," I said. "I can tell you're not doing well." I turned to Bo. "I might take Titan back —I only had another hour scheduled, but Kylie and Jimmy should be fine here on their own. I'll swing by to close up when they're done, since I know you're taking Summer out to eat tonight."

Bo looked skeptical, but Kylie pointed us to the gate. "You two go on home. We can handle things here —it seems slow today, anyway."

Jimmy moved behind the counter, so I wrapped a supportive arm around Titan's waist. He let out a slight groan and looked down at me. "I have to admit, the ibuprofin isn't cutting it." He sneezed several times, then added, "I think I need an allergy pill, too. Would you mind helping me out to my car?"

I wrapped my other arm around him. "I'd be happy to, Sir Titan."

AFTER TITAN AGREED to drop by my place for an allergy pill and large ice pack, I slowly drove out of the fairground, watching him follow in his SUV. I swerved wide for the potholes, so he'd know to avoid them. The last thing his aching body needed was more jolting.

When we pulled up to my curb, Titan parked behind me. As he eased out of his black SUV, he kept his jaw clenched, so I knew he was in pain. I ran over to help him to my back gate.

Waffles started barking in her yard, her curly head repeatedly popping above the fenceline as she jumped up to spy on us. Titan finally cracked a smile.

"That dog is completely nuts, isn't she? But good company for Vera, I'd imagine."

I helped him dodge my overgrown azalea bushes, wishing I'd taken time to trim them back. Nodding, I said, "If not for Vera, I'm fairly certain Waffles' final shelter visit might have been her last. She was a repeat visitor, that's for sure. Several people actually adopted her, but then returned her when she didn't adapt to their homes."

"Vera had the magic touch, then." He grabbed hold of my porch post in order to lug himself up the steps.

Coal stood ready to greet us as I unlocked the door to let Titan through. He headed straight for the couch and collapsed onto it. His feet protruded over the end, and it struck me that both my dog and my boyfriend were jumbo-sized.

I brought him the ice pack before retrieving some extra ibuprofin, an allergy pill, and a glass of iced sweet tea, which I set on the coffee table. Once he had settled the pack behind his back and taken his allergy pill, he released a huge yawn.

"Would you mind if I rested here for a little while?" he asked.

"Not a bit. You deserve it, after your smashing performance."

He gave me a quick look. "I didn't make a fool of myself out there, did I?"

I gently rested my hand on his strong shoulder. "Not at all. You were dapper and valiant. The crowd probably thought you've been riding horses all your life."

He sighed and leaned back into the pillow. Coal wagged his tail and scooted closer, stretching out next to the couch as if ready to cushion Titan if he fell.

"And this dog is worth his weight in gold." Titan gave Coal's head an affectionate rub. "You couldn't have asked for a better-natured canine companion."

"Ain't that the truth," I said, heading to the kitchen to grab a treat for Coal.

Titan drifted off to sleep almost immediately, so I quietly puttered around, cleaning counters and getting rid of expired foods in my fridge. Once an hour had passed and Titan was still conked out, I wrote a note letting him know I was heading to the fairgrounds to close our booth, and I directed him to some frozen eggrolls he could heat in the air fryer if he needed a snack before I got back.

Coal didn't seem the least bit interested in going out, so I left him lying in front of the couch while I locked the door behind me. His loyalty to Titan was as strong as his loyalty to Bo, and I loved seeing it, because I didn't want to marry someone Coal didn't like.

And, once again, I found myself thinking about marrying Titan. It seemed to happen frequently of late.

As I got into my SUV, it hit me that Titan's sole motivation for jousting might not have been limited to helping Cora out of a pickle. Maybe—just maybe— he'd done it to impress me. To show me what my knight was capable of.

The thing he didn't realize was that he'd already proved himself to me, again and again. I would never be able to refuse if he went so far as to ask for my hand in marriage. Although some small part of me worried that I wouldn't be prepared for it, the larger part assured me that marrying Titan would launch me into the most fulfilling years of my life.

15

J immy and Kylie had cleaned up the coffee area before they left, so all that was left for me to do was to load up sandwiches in a cooler to take home. Charity would drop by early tomorrow morning and place fresh sandwiches and desserts in the mini fridge, then Bo would arrange them in the countertop display.

August was scheduled for work tomorrow—alongside Milo. I wasn't at all convinced they'd manage to keep things civil, but at least Bo would be here to keep the peace.

Bristol had certainly seemed stunned to discover that August had liked her for years. I wondered if she had given him a call after her shift today. If she had, what was going to happen to her relationship with Milo?

Like Kylie said, our cafe life was starting to feel like an episode of *Days of our Lives*, and I didn't care for the drama. The fairground itself had enough twisted dynamics to keep everyone occupied, from Cora and Eli openly despising Robbie, to Robbie's terrorizing the entire female population, to Deanna's pulling him aside to warn him of his impending doom.

But where did the short knight fit into things? I had to assume he was part of what seemed to be a secret society sporting lion tattoos, but it was anyone's guess as to what that society's purpose might be. My great-uncle Clive had been a Mason, but he'd never told anyone—even Auntie A—what the Masons actually did in their meetings.

And the Phantom woman's voice had seemed so familiar. Where would I have run into her? At the cafe?

I glanced at Arlo's booth, and he gave me a friendly wave. Slinging a worn messenger bag over his shoulder, he said, "Hi, there, Macy. Your copy of *Sense and Sensibility* should be arriving at my shop on Monday. You want to drop by then?"

"I'd love to," I said. "I'll take any excuse to come over and check out the books."

He nodded and headed toward the gate. "See you then."

As fairies, mermaids, and other fairground workers streamed past me toward the exit, I caught sight of a familiar knight heading the wrong way. He was scurrying toward the forest, only to get waylaid by the Phantom, who was heading down the hill. Once they started to chat, I took the opportunity to jog closer, even though I had to keep shoving my silky dress straps back up my shoulders.

I felt convinced that the knight held the key to Robbie's murder. He'd run from me when I'd tried to talk with him, which only incriminated him more.

So how did he know the Phantom?

Dusk was streaking the sky as I finally rounded the curved hill, which placed me on the same level as the Phantom and the knight. But, in the same instant, the knight turned toward me, then bolted into the forest.

The Phantom didn't wait around, either. She scurried away from me, toward the lagoon. I'd probably have a better chance of catching up with the knight in his unwieldy armor, so I took off after him. I got a few strange looks from stragglers making their way toward the gate, but most everyone had packed up for the night.

In the fast-darkening forest, I lost sight of the knight, so I halted to catch my breath and listen for creaking metal. I saw something white ahead of me and peered closer, only to realized it was a plastic skeleton, shackled to the bars of a small square cage.

I'd stopped right in front of the torture device exhibit.

As I glanced over some of the heinous contraptions, bile rose in my throat. Given that I'd once passed out at the sight of blood, I needed to get out of the torture area, since my imagination started filling in the blanks as to how it would feel to have your body wrecked from the inside out.

I stumbled toward the right-side path, hoping the knight had continued in the same direction. Thankfully, when the theater stage came into view, I caught a glimpse of metal armor around back. The knight might have returned to retrieve something—possibly something he'd stashed behind the stage the last time I'd followed him.

Why hadn't I thought to check there after our previous encounter? I supposed Coal's extreme thirst had distracted me. But now I had the opportunity to pick up where I'd left off—once the knight left.

I tucked myself behind the thick trunk of a maple tree, thankful I'd chosen a dress that blended in with the green summer leaves. The knight threw a glance into the darkening forest, but didn't seem to notice me. Satisfied that he was alone, he picked something up and examined it in his hands.

Unsure what he was looking at, I pulled out my phone camera and zoomed in on the object. As I'd suspected, he held a green metal water bottle, exactly like the one I'd seen Robbie hand him before his final joust.

It had to be the conduit for the fatal eye drops.

I needed to know who this deadly knight was so I could steer police in the right direction. They were way off course if they were still looking into August as a suspect.

A breeze whipped along my arms, sending an unexpected shiver up my spine. Following a strange hunch, I pulled up my camera lens again, this time focusing on the knight's shorter build.

Had I been overlooking the obvious?

Was it possible the elusive knight was *August*?

Before I could process that idea, he started walking toward the main path. He never looked my way, so I had to assume I was hidden enough off to the side. I held my breath, trying to blend in with the foliage.

There was an off-chance that he would take his helmet off, especially since he'd just done some running in it. If he did, I might be able to catch a photo of the man who had poisoned Robbie.

As he drew closer, he absently veered left—toward me. If he continued in the same direction, I'd be completely exposed.

I backed up...only to run into someone standing directly behind me.

I whirled around to apologize, but wound up gasping in horror. The plague doctor, complete with red eyes and grasping talons, took a step toward me— looming so close that his gnarled black beak nearly touched my hair. In one swooping, birdlike move, he flung his arms out to the sides and extended his clawed fingertips, making a grab for me.

Letting out a breathy screech, I dodged his grasp before tearing willy-nilly through the shadowed woods. I hoped I wouldn't smack into a tree and knock myself out, but my hours spent in the woods in my younger years seemed to play in my favor, alerting my senses as to when an object was in my path.

The trees opened up, and I cast a wild gaze around the darkened fairground, trying to get my bearings. The lights on the hill where I stood had been turned off. A couple of lights glimmered down by the front gate, but they seemed impossible to reach. Clouds had covered the sliver of moon that was out.

Before I could take another step, rain spat at my head. A light mist started to rise from the ground, which further obscured my view.

The plague doctor charged through the leaves behind me, his breath heavy with exertion. I'd hoped I could outmaneuver him since he was so big, but somehow he'd managed to keep up. I needed to make a snap decision and move.

Praying I wouldn't tumble into the lagoon, I hurried forward. It would help if I could use my phone light, but that would only serve as a beacon to my dogged pursuer.

I slowed, sensing I was coming up on something big. A gray wall loomed before me, and I could make out a wooden door tucked into it. In an unsettling twist, I'd managed to stumble upon the castle maze that I despised.

There was no way I could detour around the wide building before the hideous, red-eyed fiend descended upon me. I tried the door handle, only to find it had been unlocked. Unsure if I should feel relieved or terrified, I headed into the darkness, quietly closing the door behind me.

With outstretched hands, I felt my way forward.

Each turn seemed to take me deeper into the belly of the castle. To my dismay, I heard the wooden door open and someone step inside.

My flight response urged me to hurry, but I forced myself to slow down so I wouldn't wind up bashing into a wall. Light bounced around a corner, and I realized the plague doctor was using his phone to light the way. He would reach me in no time.

The maze was totally unfurnished, so I had nothing to hide behind, save some plastic ivy crawling along one wall. Even a pile of ivy wouldn't manage to hide my entire body in a believable way.

Knowing I was beaten, I sank to the floor and pulled out my phone, ready to place a desperate call for help. But before I could even enter my keycode, a white light blinded me, and the plague doctor jogged over to my side.

I attempted to scream, but a strangled cry was all that emerged from my anxiety-parched throat. Before I could try again, the relentless creature ripped off one of his long, clawed gloves and stuffed it in my mouth, then tied the other around it and knotted it on the back of my head.

In a deep, gruff voice, he commanded, "Stop nosing into Robbie's death. He was a terror to women, and he had it coming."

As he grabbed my arm and yanked me to my feet, my phone bounced onto the ground. I scrambled to grab it, but he stomped on it with his booted foot.

"Come on," he demanded, pulling me forward. "You

need a lesson on staying out of business that doesn't concern you." Holding his phone aloft, he deftly led the way out of the maze. I had to admit his navigational skills were impressive, even though I still despised his steely grip on my arm and his dirty glove in my mouth.

We emerged into the fog, but that didn't deter him from his mission. Yanking me along by the arm, he strode toward the main path, as if he knew exactly where he was going.

He was leading me back into the forest.

I started struggling in earnest, knowing it didn't bode well that he was dragging me away from any employees who might still be around. But I was no match for his strength.

My worst fears were realized when his light shone on a plastic skeleton that had been pinned by its wrists to a tree. He had brought me to the torture devices...and I felt certain he knew how to use them.

16

I tried to scream against the glove gag, but my voice came out muted. Using my tongue, I shoved at the material in my mouth, managing to dislodge it a bit. Unfortunately, the tightly tied glove prevented me from spitting it out completely.

The rain had let up, but it was still drizzling, so I had goose bumps under my thin dress. If only I'd taken the time to change before driving over.

Where was Titan, anyway? He'd once told me that he always slept soundly, especially when he'd experienced growth spurts during his teen years. That might mean he wouldn't wake for some time, given his level of physical exhaustion and the allergy pill he'd taken.

It was possible that Coal might figure out that I'd been gone longer than usual. If he did, he might try to nudge Titan awake.

But it didn't help to sit around wishing Titan would rescue me. I needed to focus on the here and now.

And right now, the plague doctor was shoving me past the cage. This seemed a surprisingly promising development, but before I could breathe a sigh of relief, he aimed his light toward the wooden stocks. "You'll be going in there."

I stared at the latch on the stocks. It was placed just out of reach, so the victim would be locked in. I couldn't wind up stuck in that contraption overnight. I was already cold, tired, and hungry, and I didn't have the strength to stand that long in the rain. My legs would give out, placing a huge strain on my arms and neck.

This guy was heartless. I wished I could rip that creepy mask off his face.

Filled with righteous anger, I twisted in his grip and tried to kick at his shin, but it was of no use. He was far too bulky for me to fight. Without much effort, he grabbed me, turning me back toward the stocks.

"Get in," he demanded.

He left me no choice, holding me firmly until both my hands and my head were situated in their respective holes. He flipped the latch, and I tried again to shout against my gag. He didn't seem to have any intention of taking it off me, which would make it difficult to breathe.

He glanced at his phone, as if he had better places to be than my appointment with death. Without another word, he strode off, leaving me in total darkness.

Panic crept up my cold neck and down my bare

arms. I tried to think of comforting things, like the warmth of Coal's fur pressed against my leg, or the golden flecks in Titan's eyes when the sunlight hit them. But my brain wouldn't allow me a reprieve. It was in full-on flight mode, and I couldn't even flee.

I attempted to dislodge my glove gag by rubbing the back of my neck against the board. The tied glove gave a slight shift. Fueled by fresh hope, I continued rubbing until the outer glove slid down my chin, allowing me to thrust the interior glove from my mouth.

"Help! Help me!" I yelled, but my voice seemed to get swallowed up by the surrounding fog and trees. Would anyone be around at this hour?

A weighty silence fell as I waited for a response, but none came. The latch was on the opposite side of the stocks, where my fingers couldn't reach it. Who was the total sadist who came up with this type of punishment, anyway?

A faint electronic tinkling drifted my way from the general direction of the maze. Someone was probably trying to call my crushed phone.

I struggled to slip my hands out of the stocks, but they were locked in tight. Something clanked in the distance, so I paused in my efforts to listen. The clanks sounded like they were moving my way.

I was guessing that the short knight had stuck around the fairground. Whether that would prove to be a good or a bad development, I couldn't tell.

Sure enough, a tiny beam of light edged through the fog, and the knight came into view. But as the light bobbed closer, I realized he wasn't alone.

Three figures were moving my way, murmuring amongst themselves.

Suddenly, one woman's voice rose above the rest. "I told you, we're not about harming women," she scolded. As her phone lit the forest floor directly in front of me, they all came to a stop by my stocks.

If I hadn't been so terrified, I would've laughed at the ghoulish gang that had converged upon me. The Phantom was carrying the light, and the short knight was hunkered next to her, helmet still in place. The plague doctor was pulling up the rear.

These three could've stepped straight out of a Halloween party.

Without a word, the plague doctor circled around the others, moving straight toward my stocks. Surely he wouldn't kill me in front of the others, especially after the woman—whoever she was—had told him not to harm me. He stooped down and picked up both gloves from the ground before moving toward my head.

I braced myself and closed my eyes, but then I heard the latch flip on the back of the stocks.

The plague doctor pulled the heavy board off my head and hands. "Don't you dare make a peep, or these gloves are going back in your mouth," he said. "Now you're going to follow us."

The Phantom spoke up, and I recognized her as the woman who'd scolded him earlier. "Don't be so harsh. She's just been curious, and that's no crime."

She sounded like the one in charge. She and the knight circled behind me as the plague doctor started leading me down the hill. I hated to leave my phone behind, but I didn't dare suggest the plague doctor retrieve it for me. The sooner I escaped this bizarre situation, the better.

Once he'd led me around the jousting ring, I realized he was directing me toward the Barks & Beans booth.

He must know exactly who I was, which was more than I could say for him. Still, I had the sneaking suspicion I recognized both him and the woman, only I didn't know how. They worked as a team...like Eli and Cora, perhaps?

But who would the knight be?

I needed to find out, in order to clear August's name. Or if, on some off chance, August happened to *be* the mystery knight, I'd have no compunction about pointing Detective Hatcher his way.

"Stay here until we're gone," the plague doctor ordered. He wheeled around and started heading for the front gates.

In the meantime, I took a step toward the knight, who had lingered behind. "What are you going to do with that water bottle? I saw you with it," I whispered.

The knight creaked an arm, almost in a shrug. "That's none of your business."

I froze. Like the Phantom, the knight was also a woman, but her voice was muffled by her helmet. I wasn't sure if I'd ever met her before.

Struggling to maintain some veneer of composure, I spoke more forcefully. "It *is* my business, since police are looking at one of our employees for murder. I don't want someone innocent getting hauled off to jail."

The plague doctor stopped and reeled back a little, but the Phantom grabbed his arm. "Let's get out of here," she urged, shining her light toward the exit.

As the two walked away, the knight began to follow. But just before she reached the gates, she turned back to me. "The truth will come out. That's all you need to know."

I CONSIDERED PICKING my way through the dark to look for my phone, but I'd probably get lost in the maze, so it would be better to head on home. At least I'd stashed my SUV keys behind the counter, so I could probably make it to where I'd parked without running into the three masked amigos along the way. As I shoved the keys into my dress pocket, I heard bracelets rattling nearby.

Relief washed over me as I realized I wasn't all alone on the fairgrounds. Deanna must be around somewhere—maybe at her tent. I stepped onto the dimly lit path, letting out a squeal as I nearly ran into someone.

It took me a moment to register that it was Deanna. Her bright hair was pulled back in a braid, and she wore round glasses and silky pink pajamas. She'd pulled on fleece-lined boots and a thin robe, as if she'd been in a hurry.

"Macy! I thought I heard someone milling around over here. What are you doing out this time of night? The fair closed over an hour ago, after the last show." She gave me a once-over, her eyes widening at the sight of my hair, which had random strands escaping the high knot. "You look like you've been through it, honey," she said.

A breeze picked up, and I wrapped my arms around myself, shivering. "I got wet, and now I'm freezing," I admitted.

She stepped over to wrap a comforting arm around me, and the smell of vanilla body lotion wafted my way. "Why don't you come back to my tent and warm up? I have plenty of blankets, and I can make you some hot tea. I keep my electric kettle on all the time. Plus, I have some fresh sugar cookies I bought from my friend Sadie's booth."

Blankets, cookies, and tea sounded like the perfect way to decompress from the ordeal I'd just been through. Plus, a visit would put distance between me and the ghoul gang before I headed to the parking lot. I accepted her offer and followed her toward her tent, where a lone solar lantern sat on the outdoor table.

She opened the tent flap, revealing a remarkably

well-furnished space. It had a wooden floor covered with a plush white rug, a green velvet settee draped with a crocheted afghan, and a pillow-strewn daybed tucked into a corner. Predictably, a round table with an ornate crystal ball sat in the center of the space.

I was starting to get the bigger picture. "Do you stay here during the fair?" I asked.

She nodded, dropping a tea bag into a mug and pouring hot water over it. Then she set a cookie on a plate and handed it to me. "It's so much easier. My tent and furniture can pack right into my trailer, then I haul everything back to my place in Mason County." She waved toward the settee. "Please, sit down and pull that afghan over yourself. My mother-in-law crocheted it for me years ago, and it's the perfect thickness for these damp summer nights."

It was the perfect opening to gather more information. "Your mother-in-law—by that, you mean Robbie's mother?" I asked.

"Yes." She took a big bite of cookie, then placed it in a napkin in her hand. "To be honest, that blanket was about the nicest thing she ever did for me. Once I married him, all bets were off. I became the enemy, and that sure didn't help things."

I quietly asked, "Did you and Robbie have a bad relationship?"

She sat down and stared at the crystal ball, as if she could peer into her past. "He was no trophy husband, I'll give you that. But he cared for me as much as he was capable of, I suppose." She absently smoothed her hand over the ball. "Now tell me, why did you stay so late? Is the cafe booth really difficult to close up?"

After taking a fortifying sip of cinnamon honey tea, I explained that I'd followed a suspicious person into the forest when everyone else was leaving. "It was a short knight who kept trying to give me the slip," I said.

She seemed to follow my train of reasoning. "You thought that he had something to do with Robbie's death."

I nodded. "Only I later discovered the knight was a woman. When I followed her, she led me to the theater stage, where she took out a water bottle she'd hidden. I feel certain it's the one I saw Robbie drinking from, just before his final joust."

She gave a wondering shake of her head. "You're definitely onto something. But what happened next? Did you approach the knight?"

I filled her in on the rest of the story, from the plague doctor to the arrival of the knight and the Phantom when I was trapped in the stocks.

Deanna held up a hand. "Wait—the Phantom of the Opera? Are you sure?"

I suddenly recalled that she'd spoken with the Phantom earlier this afternoon, at her tent. "I've only seen one Phantom around here. Do you know who she is?"

She took another bite of cookie, chewing it slowly. "No, I don't, but she dropped by my tent for a palm reading today. She left her umbrella behind, so that's why I came to your booth and asked her to drop in. She'd told me she was from out of town, so I doubted she'd come back for it tomorrow. But it was a nice umbrella, with one of those wooden handles."

I shifted on the settee, pulling the afghan tighter around my shoulders and sipping the now-lukewarm tea. I wanted to get home before Titan woke up from his medicated stupor, so we could grab some supper together on his last night here. "Thanks so much for the tea and the cookie," I said. "I'd better get on back, since my phone is lost in that maze somewhere, and my boyfriend will be wondering where I am."

"You'll call the police, too, I would hope?" she urged. "They should be aware there's a killer running around on the fairgrounds. I'll certainly be keeping an eye out for that knight and the others myself."

"Good idea." Unfortunately, if they decided to go on the run after what they'd done to me, the incriminating water bottle would never be found. I sighed, and Deanna walked over and patted my shoulder.

"Would you like to borrow a jacket before you head home? It's still misty out there. I can walk you to the gates, but you can let yourself out, since they lock from the inside."

I'd been wondering how my pursuers had managed to walk right out after the gates were closed for the night, and that explained it. I stood, holding out my mug and plate. "Where do you want me to put these?"

She took them from my hands. "I'll set them in my wash tub over in the corner."

As she padded toward the basin, I noticed a crunched-up Barks & Beans Cafe cup tucked into the side of her brown tote. "Did you wind up trying one of the drinks from our faire menu?" I asked. "I thought you didn't drink coffee."

She whirled around. "Oh, yeah, I got a latte. It was great." Out of nowhere, her tone had taken on a chilly edge.

I glanced at the cup again, trying to understand her sudden change in demeanor. She had been quite adamant about hating coffee, so why would she have bought a latte? It felt like she was lying, and about a used cafe cup, of all things.

The truth crept up and smacked me in the face. Deanna was lying because that *particular* cup was significant, and there could only be one reason that was the case.

It had to be the cup Robbie had drunk his chai latte from on the day he was poisoned. The cup he'd carried right into her tent, when she'd invited him in to read his cards.

How easy would it have been for her to dim the lights, retrieve an eye drop bottle from her bag or even her pocket, then squeeze a few drops into his latte? It didn't take much imagination for me to visualize the entire event playing out in the shadowed tent.

I tried to rein in my hasty conclusions. Maybe someone had simply dropped a cup in front of her tent, and she'd shoved it in her bag to throw away later. Or maybe she'd actually tried a latte, just like she said.

She turned from her dish basin and walked my way. "Let me grab that jacket for you," she said cheerily. She scooted around me, then reached into a basket by the door.

As she extended her hands, her sleeves edged up, revealing a small lion tattoo on her right forearm. I blinked to make sure I was seeing it correctly. It was definitely a maned lion, like the others I'd noticed.

If Deanna was also part of the secret society, she could be in league with the tattooed knight—even protecting her, like the plague doctor had.

Her benevolence toward me tonight might've been a complete façade. It would have been easy for her to fake alarm over my story, then invite me into her tent —the same way she'd invited Robbie in.

Had she put drops on my cookie or in my tea? I tried to recall if there'd been a moment I'd turned my attention away as she'd prepared my food.

I tried to talk myself down. I felt fine so far. Robbie had experienced respiratory distress, and my breathing seemed normal. But maybe respiratory distress didn't announce itself.

If Deanna *was* in the society and had been involved with Robbie's murder, it followed that she'd have no intention of letting me go. She already knew I was planning on contacting the police about what I'd been through tonight, and now I'd seen her coffee cup, as well.

She was going to have to silence me.

I looked at her as she straightened up. It was probably no accident that she'd positioned herself in front of the tent flap I needed to use as an escape.

When she turned to me, bracelets jingling, it wasn't a jacket that she was holding in her hands.

It was a large kitchen knife.

17

I wasn't the best at thinking up escape plans on the fly—that was Bo's forte—but he'd taught me several self-defense moves. For instance, when you were presented with a knife, your best option was to distance yourself from said knife.

I took a step back, holding up my hands. "There's no need for this."

Her eyes narrowed. "I'm sorry, honey, but there is. You can't go blabbing about that cup to the police." She gripped the wide knife handle and stepped closer. "You're a little too nosy for your own good, you know that?"

It was now or never—I had to make my move. And I wasn't going out through the front door, like she would expect. Bo had also taught me about the importance of surprise.

I turned and ran as fast as I could into the back of the tent. Slamming into the taut waterproof material, I kept running until the entire thing collapsed on top of my head.

If I was going down, I planned to take Deanna down with me.

To my surprise, the bottom of the tent pulled up, exposing an opening onto the wet grass. I managed to crawl out from under the cumbersome material, then took off running toward the gate. If only I could make it to my SUV, I could take off, because the keys were still in my pocket.

As I passed our cafe booth, I heard the sound of fabric ripping. Without turning to check, I knew Deanna had managed to hold onto the knife when the tent fell, and now she'd cut her way free.

I flipped the deadbolt on the gate and tore out, not bothering to pull it shut behind me. The grassy lot was lit by two LED floodlights, and most of the cars were gone, so I instantly spotted my white SUV. I dodged a van and an old Volkswagon bug, racing toward it. But just before I reached my driver's side, I heard the metallic thud of another car door. I managed to yank my door open, but before I could get inside, someone had jogged up and grabbed me.

I let out the loudest scream I could, struggling to break free of the person's strong arms. To my horror, a familiar gloved hand wrapped around my mouth.

It had to be the plague doctor.

As he yanked me against his torso, all doubt was removed when his beaked mask protruded over my head. He must have been lurking in the parking lot all this time, waiting for me.

What kind of an organized gang was this? They had people everywhere. Even now, Deanna was probably racing our way, planning to kill me.

My unrelenting captor started dragging me backward, so I dug my heels into the grass and tried to bite his hand. I didn't get far, since the bulky glove prohibited skin contact.

I heard the roar of a vehicle, then a black SUV came flying down the dirt drive. It cut onto the grass and headed straight for us. If I hadn't recognized it, I probably would've fainted from fright that it was going to plow us over. The plague doctor must've had the same impression, because he gave me a hard yank, trying to force me to move faster.

The SUV pulled to an abrupt stop, then the door opened a crack, allowing an impressive-sized gun barrel to point through it. A deep voice shouted, "Get your hands off her now."

It was a beautiful voice, and a voice that meant business. It was the voice of my avenging boyfriend. He'd never used that authoritative tone with me, but it was equal parts commanding and hypnotic. I dared anyone to defy it.

The plague doctor did as he was told, dropping his hands and allowing me to stand. "I didn't plan to harm her," he said.

Titan stepped out, gun still aimed at the masked

man. He motioned for me, and I raced toward him, positioning myself behind his wide back.

In a surprisingly polite tone, the man asked, "Do you mind if I take off the mask?"

Titan had nothing to lose, so he gave a brief nod. The repulsive plague doctor slowly removed his beaked headpiece and dropped it to the ground.

I stared at the man who'd been behind my fairground torment—Owen Blackwell. I should've guessed that he'd be in on things, given his lion tattoo.

Owen raised his hands, speaking in a strained voice. "I wasn't going to hurt Macy, I swear. My mother is in the van, and she'll back me up. We saw Deanna chasing her out of the gate with a knife, so we planned to grab her and get her out of Deanna's sights."

"But what happened to Deanna?" I demanded, frantic to know the whereabouts of the woman who'd tried to stab me.

"She saw me and ran," Owen said.

I edged out from behind Titan, who still had his gun poised. "But aren't you working with her?" I asked.

Owen shook his head. "We were trying to expose her as Robbie's killer. It's a long story, but my mother and Iris can help explain."

Iris—Robbie's first wife. The woman with the scar. She'd been working with Owen?

Titan finally holstered his gun, as if he believed Owen's story. He pulled out his phone. "Let me get some backup, then you'll have your chance to explain."

Bo was the next to arrive, summoned by Titan's call. He jumped out of his truck and jogged toward the van. I was sitting in the middle seat, with the sliding door open.

After giving a respectful nod to Titan and Owen, who stood on both sides of the van to guard it from Deanna, Bo leaned in toward me.

His serious gaze fixed on me in the semi-darkness. "Are you okay, sis?"

I nodded, giving him permission to turn back to Titan. I knew they had bigger fish to fry—namely, finding Deanna.

"Charlie's on his way," Bo said tersely. "You said we needed to look for someone?"

Titan gave Bo a brief description of Deanna in her robe and PJs, then Owen added that she'd probably run into the woods to our right, since it was the best place to hide.

Titan mentioned that she was carrying a long knife, but Bo just gave a grim smile and patted the Glock in his belt holster. "If she's around, I'll find her," he said. "When Charlie comes, you let him know my 20."

Titan nodded. I appreciated that even though he could've taken off after Deanna, he'd chosen to stay with me. I doubted he was completely comfortable leaving me alone with Owen and crew, even though they'd said they were trying to protect me.

Iris shifted in the seat beside me, her armor creaking. She was the short knight I'd been chasing.

Now that she'd removed her helmet, I could make out her distinctive cheek scar. She kept her attention focused on Owen, letting me know they had some kind of deeper connection. I recalled how she'd waved at him at the shelter, and the way he'd jumped into protective mode when he realized I'd spotted her with the water bottle. I still didn't understand what significance the bottle held, since Deanna had likely poisoned Robbie's cafe cup. But everything would come to light soon enough, once Charlie started questioning people.

Rosetta Blackwell sat in the passenger seat, looking remarkably composed as she observed the men outside. She'd removed her Phantom cape and mask, and her smooth, silver bob was lit by the overhead lights. I wasn't sure what role she'd played in things, although I appreciated that she'd been the one to tell her son to release me from the stocks.

As if sensing my misgivings, Owen leaned into Iris' open window. "I'm sorry I gave you such a scare, Macy."

Titan took a subtle step backward on my side of the van, and I could tell he was listening to every word Owen said.

Owen continued. "I overreacted because I was concerned about Iris. You stumbled into a tricky situation, because Iris had determined to tell the police she'd poisoned Robbie's water bottle—"

"That much is true," Iris interrupted.

Owen gave her a tender look. "You only used a couple of drops. That wasn't enough to kill him."

Rosetta chimed in. "It wasn't even Iris' idea in the first place. When Robbie accosted that young girl, Amber, we'd all had enough. We were trying to think of ways to shut down his repellant behavior at the fair, and Deanna suggested that she'd seen in a movie that you could use eye drops to make people feel sick. She had a bottle with her, she said."

Iris fell silent, staring at the dim circle of light on the grassy hill. Owen reached into the window and gave her hand a light squeeze, then he walked around to our side of the van and started filling us in on the details.

"Iris found an extra knight costume in the theater clothing bin, so she changed from her red fairy costume into that, to keep her identity a secret," he said.

Iris had been the red fairy I'd seen comforting Amber in the woods. I glanced her way, but she didn't seem to feel the need to explain. She continued staring out the window.

"I put those eye drops in his water bottle," she said slowly, to no one in particular. "He never knew it was me in that costume, either."

Anger flashed in Owen's eyes. "Of course he didn't recognize you—his first wife that he thought he could cut and...and *beat*...with no consequence. *You*, who were nothing but patient and loving with that cowardly brute."

Iris turned toward him, swiping at tears. Titan moved closer to the open door, troubled to see a woman in such pain.

Rosetta spoke, her tone more than a little ruthless. "He deserved what he got."

"But Iris didn't do it, Mother, and I won't let her go to prison for it," Owen said. "Deanna was the first to poison him—she might as well have admitted it when she invited you into her tent to tell you she was packing up to leave the faire tomorrow. She'd decided to make a run for it. And then you noticed that crumpled cafe cup in her bag, even though she didn't know you did."

"I was planning on telling the police about Deanna's cup," Rosetta said, "but then Iris went and derailed things by staying behind to retrieve that water bottle. Trust me, I would've never let her or August get pinned with a crime Deanna committed."

Owen frowned. "She thought she'd frame Iris with the overdose she'd already administered. She used the incident with Amber to her advantage, convincing Iris she should punish Robbie with a few eye drops. She was playing on Iris' trusting nature—just like Robbie did." He looked toward the woods, clearly thinking dark thoughts toward the conniving fortune-teller.

He didn't need to worry, though, because she couldn't possibly escape with Bo on her heels. He might already have her in hand.

Rosetta reached out the window and patted her son on the arm. "We'll give Detective Hatcher the water bottle and tell him the truth. He's a good man, and he'll get to the bottom of things." She fell silent for a moment. When she finally spoke again, her voice was charged. "Charlie helped me when I got settled in, all those years ago. He was a young officer then, but he was determined to keep both of us safe from your dad. He kept a watch on the house for several weeks, to put my mind at ease."

Iris spoke up. "I appreciate your looking out for me, Owen, but your mother is right. We need to tell the police what I did. I can't live with it if I accidentally killed someone."

Owen's face softened, allowing me to see that he wasn't all plagues and talons. Yes, he'd taken drastic measures with me to keep Iris from getting incriminated—or from incriminating herself—but he was clearly motivated by love. For Iris, as well as for his son.

Iris continued, "Deanna might not have even understood her motives, so I feel sorry for her. Like all his exes, she would've had trauma from Robbie's abuse. His behavior toward the women at the faire could've acted as a trigger, compelling her to stop him once and for all."

Owen shook his head. "But she's not without blame. In fact, I think she was quite calculating. After all, she co-owned that horse breeding business with Robbie, and now that he's dead, the whole thing will fall into her lap. It's very convenient, because I gathered that she lost her house earlier this year. Since then, she's been traveling from campground to campground, living in her tent and working fairs for extra income."

Rosetta winced. "A man like that wouldn't pay his exes a dime. He didn't care if they lived or died."

Blinding blue lights flashed over the top of the hill, and three police cars pulled up. Charlie was the first to jump out, and he headed straight for Titan.

After getting briefed on the situation, he sent a couple of officers toward the treeline. But Bo emerged from the woods, holding Deanna's hands behind her back. She stumbled our way, her eyes wide and her hair askew.

"I found her hunkered down in a field," Bo explained, handing her over to an officer to be handcuffed. "She admitted that she pulled a knife on my sister." The way he said *my sister* spoke volumes, making it clear that Deanna would rue the day she ever tried to pull that trick again.

Charlie nodded, then turned toward the van. "I appreciate your help, everyone. I'll just need to get some statements really quick, then I'll let you get home."

Bo and Titan joined the officers, ready to share what they knew. I wasn't ready to rehash my harrowing night just yet, so I stayed put.

Iris eased around me, allowing Owen to help her out of the van. She placed her tiny hand in his huge one, and together, they walked toward Charlie, like two people facing the firing squad.

Rosetta turned and spoke to me in a low voice. "Please rest assured that my son never would have harmed you. He needed you to stay out of the way so he could get Iris out of there. She was his first love, you see—back when they were teens. He doted on her."

She heaved a sigh. "But then Robbie swooped in like a proverbial bad boy and proposed to her, just one month after they'd met. It was a mistake right from the start, but Iris was headstrong, and her parents couldn't talk sense into her. It was torment for Owen to watch her endure that doomed marriage, but he couldn't convince her to leave Robbie. He wound up meeting and marrying his own dear wife soon after, then Iris wound up leaving Owen of her own accord. But not before he'd done irreparable damage to her face and her psyche." Her lips twisted.

"So you think Deanna played on Iris' emotions, urging her to put eye drops into the water bottle before the joust?" I asked, trying to get a clearer picture of the sequence of events.

"Yes—she handed the bottle to Iris and encouraged her to disguise herself, so Robbie wouldn't recognize her. But it didn't take long for Iris to confess what she'd done to Owen and me. We told her to hide the water bottle and retrieve it at some later date."

"That's when I first followed her into the woods," I said.

She nodded. "It must have been. But once Robbie died and August started to come under suspicion, Iris felt guilty and planned to confess. See, once you've been gaslit by an abuser, you start to believe you're doing something wrong all the time." Her voice suddenly choked off, making it clear she spoke from personal experience. "Owen couldn't bear for her to go through a police interrogation, like August had. He came to the fairgrounds tonight with the intention of stopping her."

"Thanks for explaining," I said. "And I'm glad you told Owen to release me. Those stocks are gruesome."

"He'll never do something like that again," she said darkly. "I saw a bit of his father in him when he resorted to strong-arming you. I promise you, I'll never let that happen again."

Owen walked over to his mother's window. "I heard you, and I agree. I won't let *myself* do something like that again. I was so angry about Iris and August and all these innocent people getting the finger pointed at them that I lost my mind. I swear I was going to let you go, Macy—just after Iris went home to rethink her confession. But then she dug in her heels and refused to leave until we let you out."

"Iris is a strong-minded woman," his mother said, chuckling. "And so are you, Macy." She turned in her seat and subtly pointed to Titan, who was gesturing toward the van as he spoke to Bo. "And you've gotten yourself a winner in that one. He's the kind of man who's secure enough to let you do your own thing, but he'll be right behind you every step of the way. I can tell."

I looked at my boyfriend, who stood like a bulwark

against anything that threatened to overtake me. It was true that he let me do what I needed to do—even when my curiosity led me into out-of-control situations. But he was always ready to intervene the moment I couldn't carry the load alone.

"I know he's a winner," I said, choking up some myself.

18

As Charlie wrapped things up, I stood between Titan and Bo, anxious to get home. Iris walked over to me, giving me a hesitant smile.

"Please forgive Owen. He didn't mean to harm you." She stole a quick look at Bo before dropping her gaze to the ground like a wounded puppy. "August really loves his new job," she murmured. "Please let him stay."

Wrapping an arm around her, I said, "He's not going anywhere. We've been impressed by his hard work." I glanced down at her hand. "I've noticed that you and Owen have lion tattoos. Deanna had one, too. What do they mean?"

Iris shot a nervous look toward Bo, as if she didn't want to say anything in front of him.

I walked her a couple steps toward the van. "Is it some kind of secret society?" I whispered.

She nodded. "I can't say much, especially in front of your brother, because vigilante justice is frowned upon by the law. But our group exists to put fear into abusers."

Now I was starting to get alarmed. Randall Mathena was in this society, and I didn't want him getting tangled up in something nefarious. "Have you poisoned people before?" I asked.

"Oh, no. That was entirely Deanna's idea. Generally speaking, we try to act as the bigger bully to bullies, if that makes sense. Most often, we use psychological warfare, like sending notes that we're watching them, or maybe giving them a flat tire—things like that."

Maybe I shouldn't even be listening to this, because Bo would definitely take a dim view of threats and destruction of property. "Okay. I appreciate the information," I said finally.

Once she'd climbed into the van, Owen closed the door and gave me a grim nod, as if he'd been the one to go through the wringer tonight. Perhaps he was forgetting stalking me in the maze and forcing me into the stocks. Bo and Titan wouldn't feel the least bit amiable toward Owen once they heard about those little incidents.

Irritated, I walked over and wrapped an arm around Titan, accidentally bumping the gun on his waist. I was happy to keep August on at the cafe, but Owen could keep his distance. I'd never feel safe around him again, no matter how repentant he seemed.

Rosetta smiled out the window as they pulled away, giving me a graceful wave. In the dim light, I could barely make out a small, dark mark on the inside of her wrist that resembled a lion.

She was in the society, as well.

Come to think of it, she might be at the very heart of it. What better way to find out who was bullying people than to run a women's shelter?

It was actually genius. She'd created a lion pride that looked out for their own, as well as those unable to fight for themselves.

I pictured Iris' scarred face. Then I thought of Deanna and Cora, who had also married a man they thought they loved, only to be abused by him.

I considered the countless women Robbie had harassed throughout the years, including a teen young enough to be his granddaughter.

And I realized I wouldn't be telling Bo anything about this secret society, as long as no one else wound up dead.

I STAYED home on Sunday to recuperate. Titan brought me food, then sat with me until it was time for him to drive back to Virginia. I was thankful his back had recovered from his jousting endeavor, so he wouldn't be too uncomfortable on his car ride.

After giving me a parting kiss, he whispered against my hair, "I can't wait to pick you up in July. I'll show you all my favorite childhood hangouts."

His enthusiasm was contagious, even though I still

harbored some trepidation about meeting his Granny McCoy.

But Titan was a man who was worth fighting for, and this Hatfield might just get a little riled up if someone tried to push me out of his life.

MONDAY SEEMED to start way too early when I headed in to open the cafe. Summer told me the entire *Psych* group had been adopted, so the latest shelter dogs were sporting names from *Gilmore Girls*. True to expectations, the poodle mix was named Emily, and the black, long-haired lab mix was named Lorelai. Lorelai kept positioning herself right in front of our window, where she looked longingly onto the sidewalk outside. The grass would always seem greener on the other side for Lorelai, I imagined.

Kylie showed up after Summer left, and she headed straight for the Barks section. "I saw on the news that they brought that fortune-teller in for the murder of Robbie Sears," she said. "Did you see anything after we left on Saturday?"

I didn't want to jump down that rabbit hole just then, so I said, "I'll tell you all about it later."

She did a slow blink. "That sounds ominous. Would you want me to make you a gingerbread latte? It's the least I can do." She placed her hand on the low divider wall, and I noticed something new on her right-hand pointer finger.

Of course, it was a maned-lion tattoo.

I pointed to it. "I take it you figured out what that secret society was all about?"

She gave me an enigmatic smile. "I have my sources."

Knowing Kylie's background, I shouldn't feel surprised that she'd been attracted to the lion society's mission. In fact, she'd probably be their best soldier yet.

ONCE THE CAFE STARTED HOPPING, I was surprised to see Milo's brother Hudson show up. He was impossible to miss—tall, blond, and dressed like he was heading out to golf in Palm Springs. The moment he saw me, he walked to where I was sitting.

"Macy, you're looking beautiful, as always." He'd left his sunglasses on so I couldn't see his eyes, but the smirk playing around his lips said he was deliberately toying with me.

Although Hudson was far too young for me, he thrilled at flirting each time we ran into each other. He was too rich to be deterred by the fact I had a boyfriend—after all, in his world, money could actually buy you love.

"Hudson, how nice of you to drop in. But your brother isn't working today."

He took off his sunglasses, tucking them into the

open neck of his aqua polo shirt. "Oh, believe me, I know. I actually came in to talk with you."

Uh-oh. I'd have to explain to him yet again that I was taken.

"Is that August Blackwell fellow still employed here?" he asked abruptly.

I squinted up at him. "What? Of course he is."

He gave a superior huff. "Macy, surely you must understand that he's not the sort you'd want serving customers. His father is extreme, protesting everything you can imagine. And Milo tells me that August is under suspicion for poisoning someone. You wouldn't want someone like that working in your fine establishment." He blinked his sandy lashes and stretched his tan arms, as if he'd just made a spectacular swing.

I stood up, even though it didn't put me at his eye level. "Hudson, I would think you're above spreading false information. August was cleared of any wrongdoing. Detective Hatcher has booked another woman for the poisoning you seem to know so much about—it was in the news this morning."

Doggie Lorelai pranced over to his side and sat in front of him, but he didn't even glance down at her. "That's all well and good," he said slowly. "But as a loyal brother, I feel compelled to let you know that Milo sees red every time he has to be around that hooligan. I'd suggest you schedule them on different shifts, to keep the peace."

"You're kidding me, right?" I asked. "You cannot—can *not*, Hudson Donovan—come walking into my cafe

and give me orders. I will schedule your brother when-
ever I please, and he can learn to work with August. It's
called being a gentleman."

Hudson gave an exaggerated shrug. "That's your
call. But don't say I didn't warn you."

AUGUST ARRIVED for work as I was gearing up for my
lunch shift. He looked infinitely relieved, probably
because Deanna had been arrested. He'd clipped his
beard close and gotten a hair trim, and he wore a
button-up shirt that gave him a surprisingly intimidating air.

He walked over to greet me, eyes shining with
appreciation. "Thank you for what you did," he said.
"Dad told me everything. I'm sorry he got so carried
away at the fairground. He's been in love with Iris for
years, even though he's been in denial about it. He
literally can't see straight when it comes to her. I'm
hoping he'll finally step up and ask her out before she
leaves town."

Denial might run in the family, given that August
himself hadn't come clean regarding his longstanding
crush on Bristol. But maybe he'd turn a corner and ask
her out, too.

I didn't really know who to root for in this love
triangle, given that both interested parties happened to
be my baristas. Milo had always been a loyal—

although sassy—employee, and August had tried to please from the moment he came to work for us.

Maybe when Bristol headed to art school it would ease tensions between August and Milo, but that wouldn't happen until fall. Until then, they would all have to work together in some kind of harmony.

Bristol came into the cafe soon after. After acknowledging August's friendly wave with a slow nod, she headed for the dog section. Her long, dark hair ran in a loose braid down her back, and she wore a hot pink shirt that made her velvety skin glow. She looked more guarded than usual, as if she wasn't quite ready to talk about her problems.

I jumped into the gap, giving her the rundown on Lorelai and Emily, who had been behaving admirably, even though Emily wanted to go outside every thirty minutes to see what was happening in the fenced dog yard. As we discussed the dogs, Bristol seemed to relax.

As I grabbed my bag to leave, she whispered, "Thanks for talking with me about August the other day. It made me open my eyes, in more ways than one." She sighed, twirling the bottom of her braid around a finger. "In fact, I realized that I like him more than I like Milo."

I took a deep breath. "Oh, Bristol. Have you talked with your mom about it?"

Her mother Della was my dear friend, and she was the kind of empathetic person who knew your emotional state before you did. If anyone would have good romantic advice, she would.

"I did, and she's the one who helped me put things into perspective. Milo hasn't been willing to commit to a relationship of any kind, to be honest. He'd rather flirt around and hint that he likes me. But I know August. He's not the type to play around. If he comes out and says he's interested, he's not going back, and that's actually what I want. Why waste time with anything else?"

That did make a lot of sense. "So, you haven't talked to August yet?" I asked. Emily jumped up on her hind legs, begging to go out. "Sit," I commanded.

Bristol stood and snapped the leash on Emily. "Not yet, but I plan to talk to him later today. I just wanted to fill you in so you'd know what's going on around here. I'll try not to make things weirder than they already are, but I can tell you that Milo isn't going to be happy when he finds out."

That was an understatement. I could only imagine the kinds of remarks he would make—even to customers—after being thwarted in love. Maybe he would even rethink his job at the cafe. But I couldn't let my mind go there.

"Let me know how things go." I met her serious, dark gaze. "It'll all work out."

She nodded, then walked Emily toward the side door. I glanced at August, who hastily turned toward the espresso maker like he hadn't been watching us talk. He could probably tell that something was up.

I felt a sudden wave of sympathy for Milo. Although he liked to act all devil-may-care, I felt sure he cared for Bristol very much indeed. But he should've stepped up and asked her to be his girlfriend, rather than taking her out every now and then, when he got bored. A woman needed more than casual appreciation.

I supposed it was time to loop Bo in on the romantic shifts in the cafe, since he counted on me to keep him apprised of personnel issues. I shot him a text explaining the gist of things, to which he replied, "Poor Milo."

That about summed it up. Both Bo and I had experienced romantic loss on a large scale, but we'd also learned that in the end, things could work out even better than you'd dreamed. Hopefully, Milo would learn from this in the long run.

19

J uly 3
I glanced around Granny McCoy's living room, taking in the tiered crystal chandelier, chintz loveseats, and jade statues adorning her well-stocked library shelves. Granny herself sat ensconced on a leather chair, peering at me with an unreadable look.

"So you're a Hatfield from down in Greenbrier County, are you?" She pulled her glasses down, as if to see me better. Her hair was surprisingly dark for her age, and it looked untouched by color.

"I am," I said. "And what about you—have you lived in the Wheeling area all your life?"

She chuckled. "No, I moved up here to be with my husband's family. I'm from Virginia—down around where Titan lives now." As she said Titan's name, her face softened. It was clear she loved her grandson.

Titan shifted on the couch, draping an arm around

me. "Macy and her brother run a cafe in Lewisburg—remember I told you about that, Gran?"

She gave a thoughtful nod. "A cafe with dogs, you said."

It was hard to tell if she approved of such a venture. Perhaps she thought it was frivolous work, but I tried to give her the benefit of the doubt.

"I had a dog I loved," she continued. "Sandy, her name was. Loyal as the day is long." Her eyes softened as she looked at me. "Tell me all about your cafe, Macy."

A smile tugged at the side of my lips. Granny McCoy and I were going to get along just fine.

CASSANDRA AND ARIADNE had organized a family outing for us on July fourth, so we headed over to Schenk Lake after a picnic lunch of grilled burgers, hot dogs, and potato salad. While Titan, his dad, and brothers-in-law and nieces rode in the swan-shaped peddle boats, his sisters, mother, and I talked about anything and everything under the sun.

Lori McCoy seemed every bit as friendly toward me as she'd been at Christmas. She regaled me with stories about Titan's younger years, including how he'd stolen a Tropical Barbie for Cass, who had wanted one desperately, then he'd had to take it back to the store and apologize.

"I gave him some money to buy it for his sister," she

said. "But he felt so guilty, he hid behind me once he'd apologized. I had to take the money from him to pay for it."

"I have that Barbie to this day," Cass said, flipping a heavy chestnut curl out of her face. "He's always been a sweet little brother."

"Except for that time when he cut my hair when I was asleep," Ari said. "I don't know how I didn't feel it. I wound up with micro bangs."

Their mom chuckled. "You were griping around about your curls, so he thought he was helping you out. Keep in mind that he was only five at the time." She patted her daughter's long brown hair. "To be fair, you've never had it short again."

Ari nodded, glancing at Titan's swan boat as it paddled under a sparkling spray of water. "He's loyal to a fault."

Cass groaned. "That's why it was so hard when Regina walked out on him after two years. She never gave him a chance."

My focus sharpened at the mention of Titan's ex-wife.

"She was a real piece of work," Ari said. "We didn't like her from the start."

Lori murmured, "Now, let's not badmouth your ex sister-in-law, ladies. We don't want Macy thinking we're a catty bunch."

Ari's sharp green eyes flicked over my face. "Macy's nothing like Regina," she said.

Cass turned her freckled face to the sky, as if trying

to absorb the sunlight. "Exactly. Macy's one of us," she said.

I struggled not to tear up. Titan's family was the gift I never knew I needed. Their dynamics were similar to mine with Bo, only on a larger scale. They had accepted me unconditionally, not only because of Titan's glowing reports about me, but also because they seemed to like who I actually was.

"Thank you," I said quietly. "I appreciate that."

Lori met my eyes with a thoughtful smile, as if she could see right into my heart. "You're very welcome."

THE PEDDLE BOAT sat lower on Titan's side as I struggled to take my seat. Once we'd managed to get our weight evenly distributed enough to start paddling, we headed out for a spin across the lake. The wind toyed with my hair, and the sky was the perfect shade of blue.

"Usually it's so hot on the Fourth," I said. "It's gorgeous up here."

Titan nodded. "We lucked out this year. How are things going with my mom and sisters?"

"Perfect," I said quietly.

As if understanding that my reflective tone meant that I was deeply touched, he reached over and took my hand in his. "Dad's got some pretty big fireworks planned for tonight. Every year, he expands his repertoire. Mom just prays he doesn't blow off an appendage."

I laughed. "Did you get your danger-loving side from him?"

"I might have, although I've learned to keep mine in check. I won't take any risks I don't need to take, even in my job."

I believed that. Titan was no wannabe who was trying to prove himself. He was experienced, calculating, and deadly when he had to be.

But he also had a heart of gold, as evidenced by the way he treated his sisters and me.

TITAN and I sat on his grandmother's quilt on a wide hill, watching fireflies twinkling along the grass. His dad's fireworks exploded overhead in a red, white, and blue display.

Titan leaned back on his elbows and stretched his legs out. "You know, I used to come out to this hill in my free time and pretend I was a knight. I used sticks and my wooden sword to fight off imaginary dragons." He turned, allowing me to see the intensity of his gaze as a firework popped. "But I never had a princess to protect, no matter how hard I imagined one. Still, I believed that someday I'd find her, and she'd be courageous and beautiful. I would gladly spend all my days loving her."

He rolled toward me, then pushed himself onto his

knees. Reaching into his jacket pocket, he pulled out a small box and opened it.

My breath hitched, and I angled closer. White lights showered overhead, so I was able to see the antique sapphire and diamond ring nestling against the velvet. It was a square, art deco style ring that captured my style perfectly.

"You're my princess," he said haltingly. "You're the one. Will you do me the honor of becoming my wife, Macy Jane?"

I clasped my hand around his, then eased the ring out of the box. Slipping it onto my finger, I said, "The honor will be all mine."

I heard his breath catch. Dropping the box, he pulled me in for a kiss that felt as fizzy and electric as the red fireworks snapping overhead. He pulled back, using both hands to smooth the hair behind my ears before tenderly cupping my chin in his palms and pressing a kiss to my forehead.

We sat in contented silence as the fireworks continued. An unreserved satisfaction started pouring into the empty spaces my divorce had hollowed out inside me, and for the first time, I allowed myself to fully accept the weight of the fact that Titan McCoy loved me.

It was the best feeling of my life.

THE NEXT MORNING, we discussed marriage plans over his mom's cinnamon rolls. I suggested that we wait until next year, since Bo and Summer were getting married in the fall. Since my birthday was in May, I'd always considered spring to be one of my favorite seasons, and Titan agreed that April might be a good time for him.

He would likely move to Lewisburg once we got married, so I could continue running the cafe. But he'd have to run that idea past his boss.

Titan's phone rang as I took a sip of coffee, and by the time he got off, he had a strange look on his face.

"I hate to pull us back to the present, but something strange has happened," he said. "My friend Julius just saw Anne Louise Moreau heading into Arlo's bookstore in Lewisburg."

"Arlo Edwards?" I asked, as if there were any other Arlo running a bookstore in my hometown.

"Yes. I think I'd told you that Arlo's history is kind of patchy, so we'll have to look into him again. But you'll need to be careful if you go in there. He might be tangled up with her somehow."

"Okay, I will." I certainly didn't want to run into Anne Louise again. Now that I recognized her, I wasn't quite sure how I'd react. I resented the ingratiating way she acted with Bo—one moment she was praising him, and the next, she was giving him veiled threats. "Why can't the FBI seem to catch her?" I asked.

"She's built herself a protective network, and it reaches into the highest levels," Titan said. "If one crime lord isn't coming to her aid, another one is. She's a regular femme fatale."

As his mother came into the dining room to offer us more coffee, she glanced at Titan. "Is everything okay, hon?" she asked.

He looked at me, and the serious look on his face vanished. Placing his hand over mine, he said, "It's definitely going to be."

ALSO BY HEATHER DAY GILBERT

Sign up for Heather Day Gilbert's newsletter at heatherdaygilbert (dot) com to find out when her next Barks & Beans Cafe cozy mystery, DOUBLE SHOT, will release!

Book Ten in the RWA Daphne Award-winning series!

Welcome to the Barks & Beans Cafe, a quaint place where folks pet shelter dogs while enjoying a cup of java...and where murder sometimes pays a visit.

Macy is fully invested in helping her brother Bo and his fiancée Summer pull off the autumn wedding of their dreams. But when a crime boss chooses the worst possible moment to settle a personal vendetta with Bo, Macy will have to use every means at her disposal to bring the truth to light...or the Barks & Beans Cafe might be forced to close its doors forever.

Join siblings Macy and Bo Hatfield as they sniff out crimes in their hometown...with plenty of dogs along for the ride! The Barks & Beans Cafe cozy mystery series features a small town, an amateur sleuth, and no swearing or graphic scenes. Find all the books at heatherdaygilbert.com!

The Barks & Beans Cafe series in order:

Book 1: No Filter

Book 2: Iced Over

Book 3: Fair Trade

Book 4: Spilled Milk

Book 5: Trouble Brewing

Book 6: Cold Drip

Book 7: Roast Date

Book 8: Shade Grown

Book 9: Knight Brew

Book 10: Double Shot

Standalone Novella: House Blend

Be sure to sign up now for Heather's newsletter at heatherdaygilbert.com for updates, special deals, & giveaways!

And if you enjoyed this book, please be sure to review online and share with your friends about this series!

Thank you!

ABOUT THE AUTHOR

Heather Day Gilbert has been a "dog person" ever since she was nine years old, when a stray dog named Brownie showed up at her family's doorstep. Growing up, Heather considered Brownie one of her best friends, and, like Macy, she's had a dog in her life ever since. Many of the dog and cat antics in the *Barks & Beans Cafe* series are drawn from real-life experiences (unfortunately, the washing machine flooding incident with Stormy in Book 4 was all-too-real).

This series is based in the real town of **Lewisburg, West Virginia**, which has been voted "Coolest Small Town in America" by Budget Travel. Heather and her husband regularly visit the quaint town to do on-the-spot research for the *Barks & Beans Cafe* series.

Heather's also an avid Agatha Christie fan, and would love to someday own all her books. Her favorite Agatha mystery is *Ordeal by Innocence*.

Heather enjoys conversing with her readers via her email newsletter, and she occasionally weaves her readers' dogs into this series as shelter dogs.

Sign up for more dog and book discussions, West Virginia photos, and all the latest on the *Barks & Beans Cafe* series at heatherdaygilbert.com!

Printed in Great Britain
by Amazon

51082318R00108